Million D$llar Web Presence

Leverage the Web to Build Your Brand and Transform Your Business

Chad Barr & Alan Weiss

EP
Entrepreneur.
Press

Publisher: Entrepreneur Press
Cover Design: Andrew Welyczko
Production and Composition: Eliot House Productions

This publication is designed to provide accurate and authoritative information
in regard to the subject matter covered. It is sold with the understanding that the
publisher is not engaged in rendering legal, accounting or other professional services. If legal advice or other expert assistance is required, the services of a competent professional person should be sought.

Library of Congress Cataloging-in-Publication Data
Barr, Chad.
    Million dollar web presence : leverage the web to build your brand and trans-
    form your business/by Chad Barr and Alan Weiss.
        p.   cm.
    Includes bibliographical references and index.
    ISBN-10: 1-59918-434-6 (alk. paper)
    ISBN-13: 978-1-59918-434-0 (alk. paper)
        1. Internet marketing. 2. Internet advertising. 3. Branding (Marketing)
    I. Weiss, Alan, 1946– II. Title.
    HF5415.1265.B3337 2012
    658.8'72—dc23   2011048750

Printed in the United States of America

16 15 14 13 12   10 9 8 7 6 5 4 3 2 1

Dedication

*With great love and gratitude to my wife, Laurel; my kids,
Sharon and Yoni; son-in-law, Hillel; and my greatest shining stars,
grandkids Dafna and Liav; I dedicate this book. My mother,
Zahava, of blessed memory, lives on in all I do each day.*

—CHAD BARR

*To my twin granddaughters, Alaina and Gabrielle—they are now
three years old, and by the time they are able to read this book I hope
it's obvious to them that Chad and I invented the internet.*

—ALAN WEISS

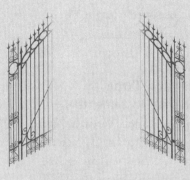

Contents

Acknowledgments

Many people dream but only the luckiest ones turn those dreams into a reality. My mentor and friend, Alan Weiss, has inspired and led me to reach the goals that I continue to set for myself. The path I journeyed has afforded me the blessing of many great friendships, which grew out of the unexpected twists and turns along the way. Phil, Guido, Kim, Libby, Stuart, and Alex along with my remarkable clients have been some of my greatest teachers. They remind me there is yet so much love, kindness, and compassion in this ever chaotic world we share. To our dedicated clients: Your desire to raise the bar is the fuel that keeps our innovative fire burning.

—Chad Barr

I'd like to thank my collaborator, technical genius, and good friend, Chad Barr, for doggedly persevering with what was a casual conversation and intent some time ago, and producing the excellent content you'll read herein. Thanks to Jeff Herman, super agent, who is constantly supportive and the most phlegmatic guy in this tough business. And my appreciation to our clients, who have utilized our services and help, many of whom graciously gave us permission to use their sites and intellectual property in this book. It couldn't have happened without them.

—Alan Weiss

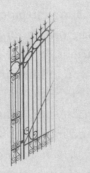

Introduction

Walt Mossberg, the highly regarded technology columnist for *The Wall Street Journal*, told us when we were together in Naples that, "No one talks about 'plugging into the electrical grid,' and, similarly, we are going to stop talking about 'going onto the internet.' We're already on it all the time."

Never before has it been this easy and risky to accelerate our brands, growth, and businesses globally. We say "risky" because the amplification that many boast about is really a cacophony, just as often drowning out the valuable while intensifying the banal. Hundreds of millions use social media platforms daily, and, at this writing, there are more than 200 million blogs extant!

Most are crap.

If you throw a rock down the street you have even-odds chances of hitting an "internet marketing expert." There are millions of pages of text, video, and audio created daily. Our intent is to take you above this fray strategically, so that you can re-enter it with a brilliant tactical plan. We've not only done this for our own businesses, but also for hundreds of clients.

It's somewhat rare for a technical and strategic expert to join forces, but we've had a highly successful relationship for a decade, and have pioneered some of the most efficacious technological and business approaches anywhere. We'll help you immediately translate your intellectual capital into intellectual property, and then accelerate its dissemination; leverage the web to enable your highest potential buyers to immediately realize your worth; and move you to a global presence faster than you can move to the next state or province.

We're going to explain why virtual communities and the reciprocating, exponential value of these communities resemble the iPhone and can parallel its growth. We'll help you become a thought leader who is respected worldwide and an object of interest to others. We'll tell you how something as simple as a Tweet can become a high-margin workshop or teleconference.

We're going to help you create dynamic Marketing Gravity™ while decreasing your labor intensity and dramatically increasing your fees.

And just to ensure that the dynamics of this world and our own ongoing creations don't outstrip this book, we're going to provide you with continual updates and new intellectual property of our own, on our sites, for you to download for free.

Sound like a good deal? You haven't seen anything yet. Read on!

—Chad Barr, Shaker Heights, OH
—Alan Weiss, Ph.D., East Greenwich, RI
January 2012

Why the Web?

what is this thing called "browse"?

The doppelganger effect

When we began working with Burst Multimedia years ago, the CEO, Jarvis Coffin, explained passionately that the web is the ultimate repository of highly qualified content.[1] What he so eloquently meant is that anyone can find virtually any specialized content quickly and easily. A New Zealander who collects Swedish stamps from the 19th century needn't engage in lengthy correspondence and expensive phone calls to find the quarry.

At this writing, the phrase "19th century Swedish stamps" yields 441,000 entries on a Google search.

For all of us in business, it's no longer "business as usual," and will never be again, which is why virtually every stamp retailer has left

---

[1] For ease of reading, we'll use "we" in all of our references even though it may have been only one of us involved in any particular client or experience.

1

Main Street and its overhead for either web-based sales or retirement. As these words are typed, people from around the globe flock to our online communities exchanging information about markets, fees, ethics, hiring, proposals, and so forth. Yet the credit and value for this opportunity accrues to us, even though we're not currently there, *because we created the community that enables such value to be exchanged.*

We have created *doppelgangers,* tangible duplicates of ourselves that provide for simultaneous relationships and ensuring value around the clock, across continents and cultures. More than mere simulacrums, the web communities enable others to engage in real time or through time shifts. We don't have to be physically present any more than a site owner has to be present while a customer places an automated order.

But our presence is felt and valued.

Ten factors of a successful web presence

What is essential in achieving your business dreams on the web?

1. *Establishing credibility.* Why is it critical for your brand and your site? Credibility is the Holy Grail of internet strategy. Most sites, counterintuitively, are not sales sites, but rather credibility sites. As we'll discuss later, that's why cheap tricks such as pop-up windows and videos that automatically start are very bad ideas.

2. *You and your business need to look world-class and demonstrate that you lead the way.* Who would want to do business with someone who looks and dresses poorly? Your site is a reflection of you. It is your virtual representation. If you don't take your site seriously, why should others?

3. *How do you stand out in the crowd, especially when everyone is amplified?* This is the fallacy of the social media platforms, which claim to "amplify" messages. When everything is amplified, nothing stands out. (When everything is a priority, nothing is a priority.) One of the best things to do is amplify your customer's voice rather than your own.

4. *How you establish credibility and incorporate its five most critical components* (see Figure 1.1):

  · *Impressive client list.* The more the better. The intent of this page on the site is to scroll down forever. We want the visitor to be positively overwhelmed.[2]

Figure 1.1: **Creating instant high credibility**

---

[2] If you are too new to have clients, you can quickly acquire organizations through *pro bono* work, testimonials gathered in public sessions, and so forth. See Alan Weiss's *How to Acquire Clients* (New York: Wiley, 2002).

- *Testimonials in both written and video format.* What should a powerful testimonial include? Name, title, organization, key challenge faced, and powerful outcomes and results. They should not be anonymous or "blind" since they are not credible then. Create a testimonial page that displays the most powerful sentence with the person, title, organization name. When possible, include a hyperlink to the actual scanned testimonial. Rotate the most powerful ones on the homepage and interior pages, and embed the applicable ones in the body of the content. Create a YouTube channel that contains all your video testimonials and then embed them into your site.
- *Case studies.* Use three simple paragraphs labeled "Situation," "Intervention," "Resolution," with a brief explanation of what you faced, what you did, and what resulted.
- *Client results*, which are substantiated by testimonials and case studies.
- *Intellectual property.* This would include position papers, interviews, models, visuals, audio, video, and so forth.

5. *The internet gives you the capability to "duplicate yourself"* (create a doppelganger) many times over or possibly exponentially, globally, by intelligently using the web and web communities. In other words, as you read or listen to this book right now, people can also "interact" with you on your online community, websites, blogs, social media platforms, shopping carts, podcasts, diagnostic tools, and so forth.

6. *Monetizing your site and productizing your business.* The more your brand is solidified, the more you can charge, until the trajectories of fee and value actually cross, and value follows fee, because people expect to get what they pay for (see Figure1.2).

7. *You need to demonstrate an impressive, proven track record or client success* so that you're irresistible to prospective clients.

8. *Who is the company you hang out with and whom do you associate yourself with?* What are your sites saying about you and those you deem to be your peers?

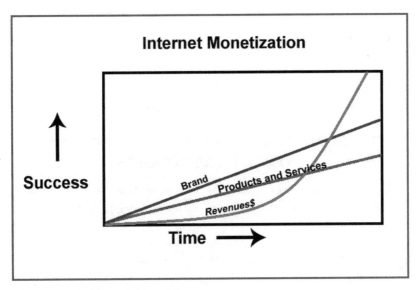

Figure 1.2: **When value follows high fees**

9. *Watch the "web trolls."*[3] More malicious than any mythical troll, they will attempt to drag you down and into their black holes to selfishly gain their own fame while ruining your credibility. What should you do, how do you protect yourself, and when should you release your own team of sharks?

10. *There is no silver-bullet approach.* Don't fall into the "if you build it they will come" trap. That only works for ball parks, apparently in Iowa or Kansas. It takes hard work, consistency, evolution, focus, innovation, and reinvention to draw high-quality customers and clients.

---

[3] These are argumentative people who insert themselves into debates, social media, websites, forums, chat rooms, and elsewhere to try to gain a higher profile and traffic for their sites by inciting interactions with others. They are mindless, but they can soil the carpets and have no manners.

Virtual Reality

Prospective buyers want to see two major things: What's in it for me, and who says so? You provide this with obvious typical client results and video and text testimonials.

HOW TO MONETIZE IDEAS

Very few good ideas are ever monetized. They either drown among a lot of other, mostly bad, ideas, or they emerge not fully metamorphosed—crystalline, fragile constructions that blow apart in a light breeze.

Here's how to turn a good idea into very good money (or at least know that it's not such a good idea):

- *Assess the size of the audience.* Do you have sufficient mass so that even 1 percent of the total constitute significant business? The "world" is never your audience. Who really might have pragmatic applicability for your product?

- *Assess the quality of your reach.* Do you have a highly popular website, lists of people who know you and trust you (or, better, who have purchased before), a blog, a newsletter, speaking appearance, alliance partners, and so on, so that your product can be projected?

- *Assess the medium.* Are you considering a form and format that is ideal for learning and use? Does the medium add or detract from your value? (Example: "Talking heads" on video rarely constitute popular products.)

- *Assess your brand.* Are you sufficiently well-known that many people will purchase merely on the strength of your name and renown? (Too many unknown people think the easy way to money is with a product. Even good products languish when people don't trust you and/or have never heard of you.)

- *Assess your price point.* People believe they get what the pay for. Are you maximizing your price based on perceived value? It's as much work to make a $10,000 sale as a $1,000 sale, so why not make the former? The key is profit, not numbers of sales.

> ## HOW TO MONETIZE IDEAS, continued
>
> - *Assess whether this is long-term business potential.* I believe that any new venture should reach six figures in a maximum of two years. Selling $25,000 the first year probably means much less than that in profit in terms of amortizing development and other costs, and the second year will probably bring even less.
>
> - *Assess your ego and motives.* Are you doing this because others have done it, or because you want a "book" or a "CD" or just passive income, or are you really providing value to others in varying ways that extends their effectiveness?
>
> - *Assess the market.* Is this fresh and new, or derivative? Do you really have new intellectual property, or is this the "Seventeen Habits of Teams Pursing Black Swans that Moved Cheese for the Soul"?

CASE STUDY
Libby Wagner, President, Libby Wagner & Associates

Libby Wagner, one of our "Million Dollar Websites" clients, proves that by dramatic success is reachable by implementing our monetization and success web presence concepts. Not long ago she called us with exaltation over a $230,000 contract with a global beverage company that was "sold" by the credibility of her site (www.libbywagner.com). *Reprinted with permission of Libby Wagner ©2011. All rights reserved.*

Marketing allure and attraction

The web is ideal for our concept of Market Gravity™. Figure 1.3 on page 8 is a gravity representation.

There is a profound difference between beating on prospects' doors, trying to convince them of how good you are, and prospects coming to you, saying they've heard of your value and are curious as to how they can work with you.

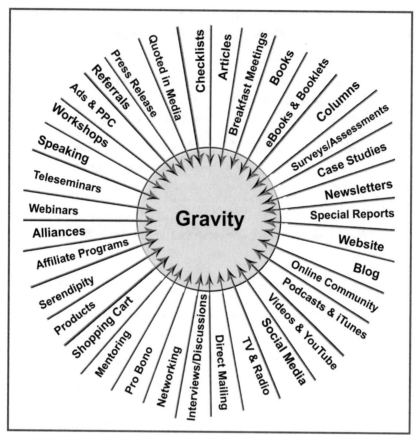

Figure 1.3: **Marketing gravity™**

In the latter case, there is zero cost of acquisition and fees are seldom an issue at all.

The secret to building a strong community of quality supporters on the web is to engage in as much of the market gravity as you can. Our advice is to begin with those "spokes" most within your comfort zone, and drill down. For example, if webinars are your passion and expertise, then find the right firms, create the right content, and market to the right audience.

Move on as you implement each tactic to those outside your comfort zone by gaining expertise and resources. You needn't use all the

TEN INTERNET MARKETING MISHAPS

1. Using a link that takes the visitor to your homepage and not to a targeted landing page. This is a huge mistake. Instead, formulate unique pages that are clear to understand with effective calls to action and direct your visitor there.

2. Not attempting to capture your visitor's information and not offering free valuable content in return.

3. Trying to do it all yourself. This applies both to your site and strategy as well as content creation. Hire an expert and partner with others for your content.

4. Evolving your content slowly or not at all or inconsistently. A great analogy that comes to mind is the one of athletes and the grueling practices they engage in to fine-tune their skills in order to get to the level of success they desire. Your practice manifests itself in the format of creating and publishing.

5. Ignoring additional effective aspects of marketing gravity and expecting your website to be the only tool to bring in business and possibly overnight.

6. Resorting primarily or only to text rather than various media options such as powerful images, charts, audios, and videos.

7. Being in love with your methodologies instead of focusing on showcasing how you help improve your clients' condition. Not realizing that your site is not about you but about your clients.

8. Looking amateurish at best rather than world-class.

9. Focusing on increasing traffic to the site rather than creating meaningful relationships.

10. Hiding behind the technology rather than using it as the vehicle to drive you virtually and physically to be with the client.

spokes (though many do), but if none of them is attractive to you, then you need to get a real job, because this one isn't for you!

There is a powerful duality present in market gravity—you attract new clients and customers but also educate existing customers about the varying ways to do business with you. This works for both wholesale

TEN INTERNET MARKETING MASTER PRACTICES

1. Leveraging your sites and technology to increase your credibility.

2. Incorporating the accelerant curve in your overall strategy of products creation.

3. Recognizing that your site is the ultimate repository of your remarkable intellectual property.

4. Effectively leveraging social media platforms and connections to build a community around your brand. Then, nurturing these connections and your community.

5. Incorporating a blog to drive content and interactions as part of your web strategy.

6. Shamelessly letting your clients rave about you in text, photos, audios, and videos.

7. Incorporating additional related resources on each page with strong calls to action to entice the visitor to click and take action.

8. Evolving with new pragmatic technologies, not for the sake of technology, but for the sake of business improvement.

9. Marketing consistently and in a variety of ways both online and offline.

10. Demonstrating passion, energy, remarkable value, and desire to help.

clients (corporations where one buyer can write a check that provides for projects engaging many people) and retail clients, where the individual consumer/user pays for himself or herself.

The more diverse your marketing efforts, the wider (and "stickier") your web. Some people enter because they want to purchase attractive

Virtual Reality

You don't need thousands or millions of hits, which is an internet idiocy factor. You need relative few *high quality* interactions. We have 20 million "connections" on LinkedIn, but no one has ever demonstrated how to earn even 50 cents from each one!

Review Questions for Clarifying Your Web Strategy

Answering these questions will provide the clarity necessary to then develop your tactics.

1. What do you want the site to do and why?
   - ❏ Create credibility
   - ❏ Deliver value
   - ❏ Educate the visitor
   - ❏ Diagnose the visitor through a process visual or survey
   - ❏ Enable products purchasing for passive income
   - ❏ Leverage marketing effectively
   - ❏ Promote your products and services
   - ❏ Promote your books
   - ❏ Capture visitors' information
   - ❏ To be fun for visitors

2. Identify your audience(s)
   - ❏ Identify all groups
   - ❏ What are their hangouts and where do they live and work?
   - ❏ What do they read?
   - ❏ What trade shows do they attend?
   - ❏ Where are they on the web?
   - ❏ What are they looking for?
   - ❏ What is their age group and sex?
   - ❏ Do they search on search engines?
   - ❏ Do they use social media platforms, and which ones?
   - ❏ Should journalists be targeted?

3. What are you known for?
   - ❏ List dramatic results you have created from your clients.
   - ❏ Substantiate results with client testimonials and case studies.
   - ❏ Think in terms of the remarkable value you provide your clients rather than leading with your resume and your methodologies.
   - ❏ What is the outstanding value you bring to your clients and what are your distinct and breakthrough offerings?

Figure 1.4: **Review questions for clarifying your web strategy**

products; others because they learn best through downloading teleconferences; still others because they read interviews; more because they populate YouTube.

Note that you draw people to you via both web-based and non-web-based options, because you never can be sure about which buyer is most influenced by which kind of gravity.

CASE STUDY
War Story, Stuart Cross, President,
Morgan Cross Consulting

Since I started my consulting business, a little over four years ago, I have transformed the way I use the web to drive my brand, my value, and my revenues.

To begin with, I had no more than a "static" website; just a few pages that gave a name, address, and telephone number. It was only when I stopped and looked around and saw what others were achieving on the web—and then immediately got some professional help!—that I fully understood its potential.

I now have a website, a blog, two e-newsletters, videos (including a YouTube channel), audios and podcasts, e-booklets, a store, dozens of articles, and am active on Twitter.

There are some "rules" that I have followed that I believe have contributed to my success on the web:

- It's about credibility, not hits. I don't need millions of people to visit my websites; I just need people who are interested in my services. The site, with its articles, testimonials, and case studies, is designed to demonstrate my credibility and give them confidence that I am someone who can help them and their business, not to generate sales instantly.

- People learn and research in different ways—accommodate them. It's not enough to have a few articles anymore. Some people prefer

CASE STUDY, continued

watching to reading, whereas others like to listen to audio downloads in the car. It's far better, I think, to have video, audio, and other forms of value, as well as articles, so that you can meet your visitors' needs however they prefer to access it.

- A steady rhythm of activity beats infrequent torrents. I plan time in my diary to write my weekly and monthly newsletters and three blog entries each week; I organize a session with my video guy twice a year to create six videos that are released on my blog and website each month; and I set deadlines for myself to come up with the content for my teleseminars and audio downloads. The rhythm of this activity means that I am constantly drip-feeding value to my subscribers, readers, and followers, helping me to stay front of mind for the point at which they may have an issue where I can help.

- Size matters, so don't let up. Over a period of four years I have created a body of work that stands up favourably to many other consulting businesses. This content has begun to help me attract new clients outside of my normal networks and relationships. Last week, for example, the director of a business, who is responsible for a new marketing campaign, contacted me. She has asked me to work with her business to create a series of strategy booklets and teleseminars, and also to coach a handful of their new customers, as a way of adding value to their own customer offer. And the specific reason she got in touch with me was the amount and range of material I had on offer on the web.

—Stuart Cross, President, Morgan Cross Consulting, UK,
www.morgancross.co.uk

Reprinted with permission of Stuart Cross ©2011. All rights reserved.

Take a quick tour around our gravity wheel. There are 33 avenues of attraction. How many are you:

Proficient in and applying now:	___
Actively trying to develop:	___
Considering developing:	___
Definitely going to avoid:	___
Uncertain about:	___
Total:	33

Our advice is that you need a minimum of 60 percent in the top two categories, and 75 percent in the top three categories. These are our guidelines, along with the best practices above, for fulfilling your web dreams and building serious business.

You may have spokes of your own to add, and that's fine. You may reinterpret some of ours. But if you believe for a moment that the "reach" and power of the internet are breakthrough opportunities for that repository of high-quality information and resources, then these are the routes that will lead people to you. You're the destination, but you can't place obstacles in the way.

Now, how do you make that destination even more attractive?

Creating a (hopefully) warm body of work

Presence on the web comprises more than your name and photo, or that abomination "website under construction," which people assume will propel prospects to come back and check on progress every day. We've seen websites under construction for a longer period than the New York subway system.

An effective "body of work" is organic. It is modified, improved, and grown as your experience and intellectual capital grows. But it should include over time:

- Position papers, which describe your viewpoints on your business, your clients, your results, trends, analyses, and so forth.
- Newsletters, which are created around a topic (narrow, such as "sales closing skills," or broad, such as "life balance") and open to wide audiences interested in that subject matter.

- Models, graphics, and other visuals, which are diagnostic and applicable to those seeking involvement and understanding of your value.
- Text, audio, and video downloads which are free, "low barrier to entry" items to attract people to greater levels of involvement. (It's ironic that the internet provides so much flexibility in media yet so many people simply default to print and text modes!)
- Examples of value: client testimonials, client lists, case studies, "war stories," and continuing additions of improved client conditions generated by your interventions.
- Product and service offerings which convey your intellectual capital and transform it into purchasable intellectual property.[4]

These are examples of building a sophisticated, comprehensive body of work on your sites. For specifics, visit www.cbsoftware.com and www.summitconsulting.com.

When visitors arrive at your site, is their reaction likely to be "So what?" and "I've heard that before," or "That's new!" and "I've never thought about it in that manner"? Do they never leave the homepage, or do they download various media items and purchase products?

Guest sources are fine to include IF they are clearly your guest and NOT representing intellectual capital that you yourself don't possess. We've seen too many sites where dozens of well-known people have their public writing, speeches, and presence quoted and recycled, in order to give credibility to the site on which they're copied. That's not your body of work, that's someone else's body of work! But if a noted thinker or leader provides an article or interview *exclusively for you*, that's a sign of your thought leadership and body of work. This is a critical distinction in creating your web presence. You're the sun, the planets revolve around you. You're not revolving around some greater light source.

How can you maximize your progress toward creating a thought leadership position on the internet? Fortunately, we've learned that you

---

[4] We like to talk about IC to IP to IB: intellectual capital, transformed into intellectual property, that generates income that's bankable!

can organize a methodical approach to generating mutually supportive material, ensuring that the work you create isn't scattered but rather a critical mass behind your expertise and its global exposure.

In Figure 1.4 we've organized a major part of your web presence into the categories of competitive (only as good as most of the competition), distinct (contains distinguishing features), and breakthrough (leading-edge and state-of-the-art). On the left column we've suggested your "action" categories from the Market Gravity chart. Now you can do two things:

	Competitive	Distinct	Breakthrough
Content / IP			
Design & Navigation			
Website			
Blog			
Online Forum			
Newsletter			
Podcasts / iTunes			
Videos / YouTube			
Products (digital) pdf/mp3/mp4/cd/dvd			
Products Booklets/Books/Seminars			
Services Consult/Speak/Mentor			
Social Media Facebook/Twitter/LinkedIn			
Webinars / Teleseminars			
Ease To Do Business			

Figure 1.4: **Internet strategic profile**

1. You can rate your current web presence.
2. You can plan your future web presence.

Not everything should be (or can be) breakthrough, but thought leadership would require a great deal of it to be. And this is why anyone serious about building their reputation and business should never settle for a formulic website that they create with a template that looks like a million others. If the basic structure is barely competitive, it will undermine everything on it.

Our experience is that true thought leaders are minimally in the distinctive category, toward the right, on half these entries, and in breakthrough on the other half. Since we've indicated that a web presence is organic and evolving, you can easily build these with clear goals over short time frames.

For example, three good position papers may be competitive, but two dozen provocative ones will take you to breakthrough in that category.

You must continue to innovate and create, to move toward the right, because simply being content with where you are will not offset the tropism to the left: New developments, technologies, perceptions, economies, and so forth will tend to drive your position toward competitive unless you are *actively* and continually producing new material to minimally hold your ground and maximally move toward the right.

Virtual Reality

Create a site that others are motivated to bookmark, return to, and tell others about by asking yourself what influences you to do that yourself.

Key mistakes

- A "cookie cutter" web presence using templates, and doing it yourself

- Infrequent updates and additions
- Lack of diversity in media
- Lack of downloads of value
- Poor or difficult navigation
- Citing expert others instead of inviting expert others

Value at the speed of light

The web allows for the potential of "instantaneous value." The combinations of media, design, and devices can captivate instantly. How do you create instant value?

- "Confront" visitors immediately with "what's in it for them," and not your mission, vision, values, history, beliefs, or extended family. Every time we see something like "We believe in the highest degree of ethics and integrity," we're moved to leave a comment like this: "What a pity, we were looking for low integrity."
- Provide rotating text testimonials (about every seven seconds), with a brief accolade and the individual's name, title, and organization. Provide video testimonials that can be played at the visitor's desire throughout the site.
- Do NOT allow for pop-up panels, or any audio or video that plays automatically without the visitor prompting it. These are annoying and drive people away.
- Use a designer to maximize color, fonts, size, shapes, photos, graphics, white space, and juxtaposition. Too many women favor pastels, which are not power colors, for example. Too many people use red as a headline color, which should be used for highlighting and emphasis only. Do NOT try to design and implement your own site any more than you would try to fix your own leaky pipes instead of calling a plumber. Neither your pipes nor your site will hold water.
- Provide typical client results, with the accent on "typical." Don't focus on methodology or deliverables, but how the client's condition is to be improved.

· Provide case studies, which can be factual with the client's permission, or an amalgam demonstrating what typically happens.

Present your products, services, and relationships in a context of outcomes and results, not inputs and tasks. Don't use fees or fee bases anywhere.

Virtual Reality

You want to be seen as a diversified resource and not a seller of commodities. It's okay to have a bookstore on the site, but don't become a general store. We all know what happened to them.

Your website is an ideal vortex to create the success cycle, as shown in the graphic in Figure 1.5.

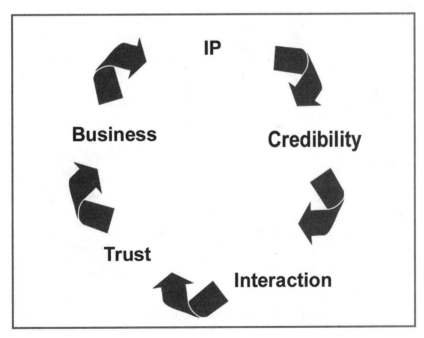

Figure 1.5: **The success cycle**

You create intellectual property, which generates credibility, which creates prospect interaction, which gains trust, which produces new business, from which you can generate new intellectual property. This sequence is accelerated by a credible website that is visitor-friendly and buyer-oriented.

As you can see in the "accelerant curve" illustrated in Figure 1.6, your offerings should range from low barrier to entry (free downloads, inexpensive books) at a "competitive" position, through distinct (teleconferences, workshops), and on to breakthrough (individual coaching, trademarked approaches), and finally your unique vault (retainers, licensed intellectual property).

"Bounce factors," such as books or online forums, allow your buyers to accelerate their relationships with you. When you have a strong

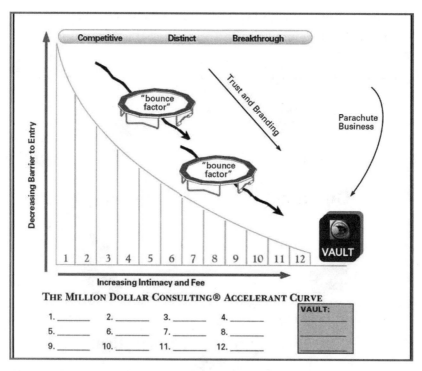

Figure 1.6: **The Million Dollar Consulting® accelerant curve**

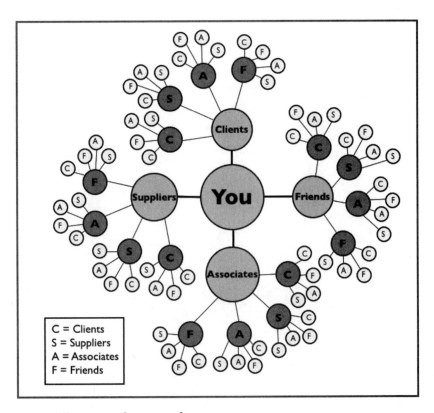

Figure 1.7: **Your connections network**

brand, "parachute business" may enter directly into the right side of your curve, *where higher fees and lower labor intensity actually coincide!*

If you were to view the potential three-dimensionally, you'd see that your connections network exponentially increases this exposure (see Figure 1.7). If you multiply the suppliers, associates, clients, and friends who relate to your business operations and goals, you will see increasing demand for your products or services and profitable relationships.

Let's take a look at how you organize to do that.

No Site for Sore Eyes

don't sell to me, provoke me

Provocative content

Content may be king, but provocative content is the ace.

You have only seconds to capture interest. Think about articles you've read, speeches you've heard, books you've begun. The initial exposure helps people determine whether they want to spend more time reading, listening, or viewing. There is simply too much competition for time to expect that people will invest too much of theirs in trying to overcome a tepid introduction.

Here are examples of provocative content.

For an accounting firm:

- Six reasons why you're paying too much in tax
- Why the top line is more important than the bottom line
- How to get your clients to offer to pay you more than you ask

For a consulting firm:

· Why planning kills strategy
· Why cause and blame are never synonymous
· Creating evergreen customers

For an auto dealer:

· Never pay for an oil change again
· How to maximize your mileage with huge engines
· Seven great auto vacations within 100 miles

Picture yourself entering a party that you merely want to make an appearance at and then leave. When the door opens, you see some old friends, you're handed a glass of champagne, and there is a wonderful aroma coming from the kitchen. You're greeted warmly by the host, and you're asked if you're interested in a wine tasting later in the evening.

You may just change your original plans. The door is your homepage; the old friends are clients you know or identify with; the champagne is the aesthetics of the surroundings; the aroma is the tempting menu items around the page; and the wine tasting is the ability to sample some fascinating and relevant offerings.

Not a bad party!

You have to be edgy, but not poke someone in the eye. You have to be willing to challenge and amuse, while not bragging or boasting. Some useful definitions:

> *Confidence*: The honest belief that you can help others to learn and grow.

Virtual Reality

Your site, and particularly your homepage, should be pro-vocative enough to be memorable and cause others to tell colleagues, "You ought to visit this site."

Arrogance: The honest belief that you have nothing left to learn and no more to grow.

Smugness: Arrogance without the talent.

Here are our musts for your site, from a content standpoint:

- A homepage with typical client results listed.
- At least one video testimonial on the homepage.
- Revolving text testimonials (at about seven-second intervals)
- Menus that include case studies, client list, position papers, biographical sketch, contact information, product and service offerings, video explanations of various offerings.
- Four-color aesthetics that include white space, photos, graphs, and appropriate fonts and sizes. Use a professional for the design.
- Refrain from "stock" pages that are templates accommodating different text. Give every page a different look. Don't keep repeating the same photo of yourself. Use "environmental" photos (e.g., shots of you interacting with others, with your dogs, and so on), not head shots.
- A value proposition that is dramatic and attractive on the homepage.

You will lose some people who have rigid agendas and inflexible beliefs when you're provocative, but that's fine. They're not your buyers in any case. No one wants to hear the 450-thousandth explanation of strategy. But a few high-potential people would love to hear, "Strategic planning is an oxymoron. Don't handcuff your growth by listening to those below you. They don't have your view or perspective."

Where do you get the provocative ideas you need to ensure that people want to stay at your party? Whether it is the compilation of new ideas for our clients' websites, developing a new piece of software or improving an existing one, arranging or writing music, or resolving a business challenge, I often occupy my mind with how to generate new ideas. So let's explore some of the best ways:

- *Read books and relevant publications.*
- *Summarize.* Use a highlighter, pencil, or a notepad to summarize your reading and document your ideas.
- *Travel.* Explore and start conversations with new people while taking pictures or videos that can become great material for your blog.
- *Be curious and observe.* Opportunities are all around us; we just have to learn to pay better attention.
- *Brainstorm with others.*
- *Engage a mastermind group or a team of trusted advisors.* Similar to the concept of brainstorming with others, being a part of a powerful mastermind group and trusted advisors is a great way to improve your ideas and creativity.
- *Invest in self-development.* A Japanese proverb says: "I will master something, then the creativity will come."
- *Internalize.* It's one thing to watch and listen to new material and something completely different when one internalizes and masters it.
- *Question basic assumptions.* This applies not just to your own assumptions but also to those of your advisors and clients. By also exploring the cause and effect, you gain new insights to arrive at the proper solution.
- *Take a contrarian view while discussing the pros and cons of a concept.* Clients hire us not to necessarily agree with them but to often question their views and basic premises in order to improve their business.
- *Develop and use metaphors.* Just as a picture is worth a thousand words, you'll find the use of metaphors to be powerful tools for articulating a complex concept in a pithy way.
- *Create a story.* Any time we take a concept that we want to convey to our audience and deliver it through the use of an effective story, it forces us to develop ideas to make it more effective.

- *Interview others.* This is a terrific way to learn, gain new ideas, and leverage effective marketing while developing new content for your website and that of the person you are interviewing in the form of audio or video podcasting.
- *Search the internet.* The key is to learn how to use it effectively, and one of the ways to do so is to ask others how they use it.
- *Social networking.* There is also a lot of shrill noise on the net, but when joining effective and smart online communities, you may

Figure 2.1: **Effective web page design**

World-class design, elegant, inviting, yet simple and innovative.

Reprinted with permission of Kim Wilkerson ©2011. All rights reserved.

quickly gain knowledge of what is being asked and discussed, and how you may be of help to others.

- *Instantiate.* "To represent (an abstract concept) by a concrete or tangible example" or simply to simplify a complex concept.
- *Teach a topic.* There is no better way of mastering a subject than having to teach it.
- *Create a process visual.* Illustrate what you want others to internalize.
- *Speak.* Similar to teaching a topic, delivering your wisdom by speaking to an audience enables you and forces you to research and come up with new ideas, while interacting with your audience, which often stimulates other ideas.

Scott Adams said, "Creativity is allowing yourself to make mistakes. Art is knowing which ones to keep." The secret to creating, developing, and innovating new ideas is to simply take action and do it. There is no better way for creating such ideas than to just schedule the time or let the magic take place when the moment occurs. It requires you challenge yourself and take risks at times or take a break and relax at other times.

Navigation that would make Prince Henry jealous

Prince Henry of Portugal was known as "The Navigator" because he routed his country's ships down the coast of Africa. Vasco de Gama's historic journey around the Cape of Good Hope to the riches of the Indian spice trade were a direct result of Henry's pioneering work.

Of no small note is the fact that Henry never went to sea and plotted all this navigation from his comfortable chambers.

You can create from your own chambers a navigational wonder, so that prospects can explore your world. The idea is to ensure that the world is known, and that the exploration is neither tiresome nor dangerous. (De Gama reached India long after Henry's death.)

If you want to project a seven-figure, world-class business (or larger than seven-figure, and cosmic-class), then your world has to be impressive and accessible. Too many sites have an alluring homepage but then a seeming game of Dragons and Dungeons as people get lost in the innards, finally closing down their browser amid pop-up windows, requirements for email addresses, and promotions.

If you visit www.Disney.com, you'll find a kid's multimedia adventure. That's not what you want to create for your prospects. Rather, you need a sophisticated business platform that demonstrates credibility and provides a high degree of value for even the casual visitor, including business applications (that we'll discuss in detail throughout this book).

Realize that your visitors can "land" at various destinations on your site. Depending upon where they originated and what links they followed, they may alight on interior pages, not your homepage. They may be seeking an article someone cited, or a recommended download, or a photo source. That means that every single page must quickly and easily identify you, your brand, and where the visitor has turned up in your kingdom. The only GPS available to these visitors is through you. Don't allow a site designer with more cutesy ideas than business savvy to create impenetrable mystery.

You want express lanes.

Virtual Reality

How many times have you sought quick information and stayed on a site because of its allure and value, and how many times have you departed quickly, frustrated by misdirection and irrelevance? In which frame of mind do you want your visitors?

You have a relatively brief span—perhaps less than ten seconds—to captivate your new arrival. Here are some quick tips:

- Enable movement to the homepage or other pages from both the top and bottom of all pages.
- Have an explanation of where they are (e.g., articles page in the resources area of the Jane Armstrong site).

- Provide an easy way to go back to the top of the page from various points within it.
- Provide incentive to go to other areas (e.g., photos, graphics, and rhetorical questions tests such as, "Would you like to see the results of our survey on accuracy of strategic assumptions? Click here.").

On your homepage, use an old newspaper concept: Print the alluring stuff "above the fold" which, in this case, means the top half of your screen page.[1] You should have a powerful "banner" on top, with your brand, any tag lines you use, and appropriate trademark protection, as an example. Keep it powerful and simple—as we've noted earlier—but then allow navigation for people to seek more detailed information "inside" so that the homepage is kept clean. If "typical client results" on your homepage draws interest, that visitor should have the option to "click here" for more detailed case studies, as an example of effective, aggressive navigation aids.

Wherever you are on your site, less *text* is always more. People are attracted to and entranced by visual cues, and the site technology allows for images converging, rotating testimonials, video and audio augmentation, and so on. For example, text describing that you grow profits is less impressive than a sales chart arrow growing through the roof as you watch it. A statement of the quality of your work that goes on for three paragraphs is inferior to three inches that display a 30-second video testimonial from a delighted client.

Don't waste people's time; it's what they have least of, and it's why people so routinely "surf" and skim and scurry. Get to the point. If people want more information, offer the *optional navigation* to get it. Invest in professional photos and graphics, and stress

---

[1] Ironically, newspapers have been losing ground since the days of radio and are dying all around us, but the web has adapted from them better than they've ever adapted from the web.

Digression

One of the worst ancillary aspects of navigation is the omnipresent identical photo that surfaces on every page "template." It's that tacky fashion photographer head shot. Ditch it. Have a photo of you and your dog, or running a marathon, or doing anything if you can't get client photos. And change the photos on every page. Otherwise you destroy the illusion of movement, and create a constant feeling of déjà vu.

"environmental shots"—photos of you and your clients at work, not the boring head shots.

Don't create navigational false hopes, sort of a radio signal that leads nowhere. Anything underlined on your site should be a true link, leading somewhere else on your site.[2] If something is underlined, then it should lead somewhere. Don't allow underlining for any other reason. If you want to emphasize something, then use italics or bold type or even larger font size. But don't do this.

Three essential elements of a successful website

Upon review of probably thousands of websites over the years, we have come to the conclusion that in order for your organization to be successful on the internet, three key elements must be accomplished to generate such success:

1. *Design*. Your site ought to be professionally designed, attractive and engaging, and be easy to navigate in order to quickly gain the visitors' attention and interest. Good use of images is important as well as the use of action shots of you with your clients.
2. *Content*. Your site must focus on your visitors' interests and address the question of what's in it for them and how to improve their businesses and lives. To accomplish this, strong content

---

[2] We firmly believe that you should *never* link people off your site. You need to live on a *cul-de-sac* on the web.

must be developed in the form of products, services, and intellectual property, while constantly evolving.

3. *Strategy and tactics.* What should the business look like and how should it position itself online? What internet components are critical to make the business a success? How should you reach and communicate with your current and future customers? Should they be able to purchase products, read articles, subscribe to newsletters, communicate through blogs and online communities?

With that in mind, review the diagram in Figure 2.2 and notice the obvious, at the points of interaction of the circles.

1. *The missing map.* This organization has a site that is well designed with great content yet no defined strategy and tactics to create

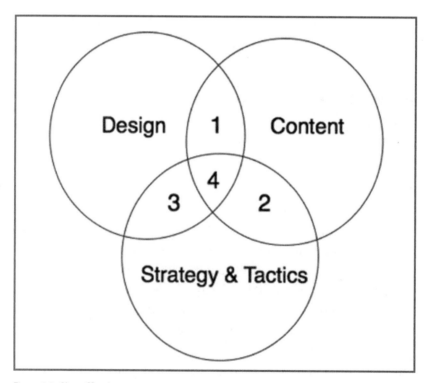

Figure 2.2: **Site effectiveness**

an internet success. It's like driving a great car without a GPS system or an effective map to follow. You'll be wondering why you are not reaching your destination.

2. *The ugly book cover.* This organization has a site that has great content and powerful and effective strategies and tactics yet the site is poorly designed and navigated. Most visitors would either close their browsers or press the back button to go to their previous site.

3. *The boring show.* This organization has a site that reminds me of going to see a theater show that was well advertised and promoted with great and colorful posters. Yet when you get to finally watch it, there is nothing there. Just a terrible and boring show. Some sites unfortunately suffer from the same syndrome.

Figure 2.3: **Combining steak and sizzle (content and design)**

4. *Success*. This organization is reaping the most benefits of effective web strategies. Any missing element and success is either delayed or nonexistent. Yet when all three circles and elements intersect that ultimate success is achieve.

Where are you? See the samples in Figures 2.1, 2.3, 2.4, and 2.5. These screenshots represent outstanding design, remarkable content, and effective strategy and tactics.

What not to optimize, organize, and legitimize

The social media advocates like to point out that the use of those platforms "amplifies" your message. Well, perhaps, but they amplify everyone's message, so that the din is merely a cacophony that is beyond deafening.

If everything is a priority, nothing is a priority.

Analogously, you can't, and shouldn't attempt to, optimize everything on your site. Here are some typical errors:

- *Attempts to tag, label, and identify every single item.* Focus on those things that are most important for your credibility. (Remember this is a credibility site, not a sales site.) If leadership is your strong suit, don't worry about highlighting blog entries on your movie reviews.
- *Use a device such as Google Alerts to let you know how you're being perceived and detected.* If your positioning is for issues that are only peripheral to your real value, then change what you're emphasizing.
- *Broken links.* We find with astonishing regularity links on large, sophisticated sites that are broken and lead nowhere. This often occurs when changes are made, *however, if no one has pointed out these errors over a long period it means no one is using the links to begin with!* They aren't central to your value and aren't of interest.
- *Extensive use of Flash, pop-up screens, automatic audio and video presentations, and other annoyances should be minimized, not optimized.* Allow visitors to *decide* whether they wish to view such promotions.

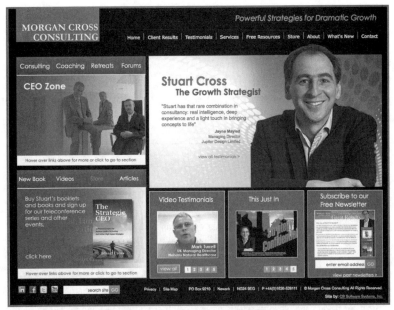

Figure 2.4: **Note the combination of personal and professional touch**
Reprinted with permission of Stuart Cross ©2011. All rights reserved.

Figure 2.5: **A varied but cohesive homepage**
Reprinted with permission of Phil Symchych ©2011. All rights reserved.

- *Mandatory registration and submission of email addresses usually drives people away faster than a rerun of The Apprentice* because of the threat of landing on mailing lists and receiving spam.

Test your site with trusted others. Don't let the public tell you that you're optimizing the wrong issues, or worse, don't let their complete silence tell you that.

Digression
The Value of Testing, from Chad

I was always intrigued by English colloquial expressions and have always loved "testing" my newly learned idioms on anyone I see in my path.

Upon my arrival to the United States (33 years ago) and during one of my college lunch breaks, I wanted to impress my American buddies with my new idioms. Being so tired from studying the night before, and while they were having their lunch, I sat down and said: "I pooped!" Their reactions and facial expressions made me realize that I may not have been clear, so I yelled again, "No, seriously, I pooped!" "Well . . . good for you, Chad!" I heard them say.

Arriving home later that evening and realizing that my new idiom had not been as effective and impressive as I thought it should have been, I decided to run this by my wife who was/ is the source of many of my exciting idioms. "You said WHAT?" she yelled. "No, you didn't!" she continued. "Honey, you forgot the apostrophe, as it should have been 'I'm pooped'!" she exclaimed.

A huge difference an apostrophe makes, eh?

The web is so all-inclusive, so efficient at finding information, that we've discovered that placing an ad to sell a car on a specialized site will result in a listing under your name when you do a Google search! But you don't want to be known as a car seller! So you need to be selective about your web "fame." That's why it's important to know what not to optimize.

Following are peripheral items, in our opinion, which might be on your site but that should not be unduly promoted and are of low priority compared to your value proposition and client results (which we'll cover in "Hitting the Buyer Between the Eyes" on the next page):

- *Links to other sites*, which we don't like, to begin with, but which you may be using out of reciprocal arrangements, sales commitments (e.g., for Amazon.com), and so forth.
- *Interviews, articles, and position papers that don't involve your current positioning, brand, or appeal.* Some people leave these on the site to create "heft" (and many simply forget they're even there), and we advocate culling them annually if they're not supporting your key strengths. But in any case, they should be subordinated and not optimized.
- *Avocations versus occupations.* This is particularly true on blogs. Many people, to create diversity or to simply engage other aspects of their creativity, will include blog items that are not related to their core business or profession. These may be political comments, or even quasi-Facebook entries such as vacation photos. (Alan runs a weekly cartoon featuring his dogs amongst his consulting advice on www.contrarianconsulting.com, for example.) However, these shouldn't receive equal treatment with the central issues of your value and brand.
- *Ego and ephemeral stuff.* Frankly, no one other than possibly your mother (and there are doubts about her) wants to hear about your mission, vision, ethics, values, or founding of your business. All of this stuff begins to look the same in any case. ("Highest ethical integrity? Too bad, we were looking for low integrity . . . .") If

Virtual Reality

Put yourself in your own buyers' shoes (or in front of their computer screens). What would take priority in terms of gaining their rapt attention, and what would bore them to tears?

you must have this on some (hopefully, buried) internal page, at least don't promote it or attempt to optimize it.

The question for you as your online entries inevitably grow with your career, success, and personal development is: "What do I ensure rises to the top? What is the cream in my career and appeal?" The Peter Principle does apply to online presence, but instead of "Everyone rises to their own level of incompetence," it's more like, "Everything rises until you can't tell the difference between competence and incompetence."

You can avoid that. If you're competent.

Hitting the buyer between the eyes

Let's review and summarize some points for high-impact web presence, and also anticipate some further issues we'll cover in the chapters ahead:

"Must" components of a high-impact web presence

- ❑ In-your-face, effective, clear design and navigation
- ❑ Strong value proposition and tagline
- ❑ Highway billboard concept
- ❑ Valuable, provocative, and useful content
- ❑ Not confusing
- ❑ Passive income products
- ❑ Secured shopping
- ❑ Easy way to contact you
- ❑ Strong call to actions on each page
- ❑ Focus on client results and successes
- ❑ Effective use of testimonials and case studies
- ❑ Newsletter registration and incentives to register for additional resources
- ❑ Ability to search the site
- ❑ Homepage above the fold
- ❑ Written from the buyer's perspective and must answer the buyer's question: "WIIFM?" ("What's in it for me?")

- ❑ Less is more
- ❑ Apps integration
- ❑ Landing pages of special reports and incentives
- ❑ Constantly evolving

What's your call to action?

- ❑ Contact us (call/email/fax)
- ❑ Sign up today
- ❑ Join our mailing list
- ❑ Purchase product/service
- ❑ Learn more
- ❑ Take survey
- ❑ Join our online forum
- ❑ Download article (white paper, CD, MP3, PDF)
- ❑ Request consultation/brochure
- ❑ Refer site/article to a friend
- ❑ Click here
- ❑ Get your copy today
- ❑ Print-friendly option
- ❑ Apply now
- ❑ Ask the expert
- ❑ View video
- ❑ Listen to podcast
- ❑ Get your score (rank yourself)
- ❑ Read what others are saying
- ❑ Like this product? Here are others you may enjoy

Don't underestimate the power of anchor text (hyperlinked words). For instance, instead of using "click here" to direct the visitor to another page, why not use a powerful and provocative sentence or the name of one of your articles, combined with a hyperlink, to send the visitor to that page?

You can add to these given the particular nature of your clients, prospects, services, relationships, and so on. For example, if you

Figure 2.6: **Hyperlinks at work**

Virtual Reality

The more I believe you have highly-targeted, distinguished value gathered particularly for me, the more likely I am to stay, mention you to others, and give you the benefit of the doubt.

specialize in high-level financial help, you could create a repository of unique resources and call it "For CFOs Only."

Some techniques to boost and monitor the success of your presence

- Allow visitors to connect and stay in touch with you by registration to your RSS,[3] email, and social media links such as Facebook, LinkedIn and Twitter.
- Make it easy to share your content (all pages) with the world by enabling social media "sharing" links such as Twitter, Facebook, LinkedIn, Digg, StumbleUpon, and Delicious.
- Ask customers, colleagues, and suppliers to create content for you by inviting them to submit articles for your blog or become a guest contributor in your newsletters. We both use guest columnists.
- Replicate your content through automation so, for example, your blog articles are posted to Facebook and LinkedIn, and the blog title, to Twitter.
- Use Google Alerts to find out who is "talking" about you on the web. When good things are said, thank them with a comment. When bad things are said, correct them as necessary. Track your name, key brands, recent posts, intellectual property, competitors, and so on.
- Use Google to find out who is linking to you as the objective is to have this number grow over time.
- Use Google Reader to subscribe to important blogs within your area of expertise, other thought leaders, and competitors. Monitor this daily for a few minutes, just as you read your daily newspaper.

---

[3] "Really Simple Syndication," which allows for notice to interested parties of any new postings and publishing on selected sites.

Always focus on the four objectives of web presence:

1. Improve and communicate your image, brand, credibility, and value.
2. Increase revenue, margins, profit, and numbers of clients and referrals.
3. Lower barriers on entry to work with you.
4. Simplify the creation and dissemination of powerful content.

The proliferation of internet "gurus" (often essentially anyone out of work) has created massive confusion about how to maximize and leverage web potential. The simple truth, however, is that your potential buyers—prospects—are "in the market" to learn, improve, enjoy, purchase, and gain—both professionally and personally, in large organizations (wholesale) and as consumers (retail). Your website is not a huge business card or merely firmware.

It is a credibility tool often exposed to those who have deliberately visited just prior to a buying decision, not usually by "trawlers" and "trollers" who are sailing the internet as if shopping in Walmart and making impulse purchases in the aisles. In your area of expertise and value, you must consider yourself, and then express your internet presence using these descriptors: best, dominant, original, leading, state-of-the-art, strongest, impressive, unique, powerful. If you want to grab the visitor's attention, you had better be focused yourself.

If you don't blow your own horn, there is no music.

And if your clients and others blow the horns through testimonials, then you have an orchestra playing in harmony, and with inspiration.

Deliver high value, be provocative, reinvent, and evolve.

 ## Why people don't use overheads on TV

When video first entered the realm of personal and professional development, via VHS and the Beta formats, it wasn't unusual to see someone talking into a camera with a bare backdrop and an easel, with a pad and markers by his side. It wasn't unusual, but it was boring!

CASE STUDY
Seth Kahan, Executive Leadership
Consultant and Change Expert

When I entered the consulting field in 2002, I knew I needed a professional website. I decided to take it seriously and designed an entire site. It featured a professional photo, description of my work, testimonials, details of my consulting and speaking, and free articles to download. I was not prepared for the authority it conveyed and the quality of responses I received.

Immediately I was propelled into a league of professionals I held in high esteem. Most consultants at the time had amateur websites they had built themselves or—if you can believe it—paid others to cobble together. Presenting myself professionally paid immediate dividends. Clients treated me differently. People shared my site widely. I commanded higher fees.

In 2007 my practice had evolved and the value I was capable of generating had increased significantly. I wanted my site to match that, so I upgraded. I never promoted the new site. I think it is silly to advertise marketing efforts. It is redundant. Nonetheless, I received kudos from many for the look and feel and the new content, over 100 free articles and videos.

The videos of my speaking engagements made a huge difference. People could eyeball me instantly and make the decision as to whether or not I was a match for their audience. The number of engagements I received climbed quickly. I was soon speaking 30 or so times per year.

In 2010 I redesigned my site to align more closely to my offerings. I put my primary activities out front. The testimonials on the front page supported my central thrust. I made it easier for people to get to the areas I wanted to promote.

I intentionally included three unique images of me on the front page because I realized that I was the product. I wanted people to get to know me as fast as possible so they could decide if they wanted to work with me before they picked up the phone. I included a professional image, a more casual stance, and a video. The reception was great. When people call me to inquire about

CASE STUDY, continued

my speaking or consulting, they almost always refer to what they saw on the website.

This last summer my book, *Getting Change Right*, became a *Washington Post* bestseller, so I promoted that on my front page. I created a little mini-site just for the book called GettingChangeRight.com. It is easy to reference. I now write for *Fast Company* and the *Washington Post*. This raises my esteem and improves my brand, so I highlight both on the opening page.

My website is without a doubt my best strategic marketing tool. I keep it updated, constantly improving it. It provides interested parties with the overall picture of who I am and the value I can provide when they choose to engage me.

—Seth Kahan, Executive Leadership Consultant and Change Expert
www.visionaryleadership.com

The trainer had simply taken his usual approach of standing in front of a class, discussing points, and drawing illustrations on an easel, and placed it in front of a camera. Not only did he fail to make use of video's additional traits—inserted graphics, animation, special effects, et al.—but he actually diminished his own classroom power by eliminating the audience, questions, spontaneity, and exercise.

Another triumph for new media!

We're in an age of media exploitation, but we mean that in a positive sense. Learning, in all its variety, can follow the example set by entertainment, with color, graphics, movement, involvement, and so forth. If you watched them change the sets on a TV drama, or had to watch people draw *The Simpsons* on an easel instead of seeing the animation, you'd probably react by going to the movies, turning on CNN, or poking yourself in the eye.

So why make similar errors on the internet?

Rules for the evolving media road

- *Exploit your strengths.* If you're a great speaker, then shoot your live, exciting, actual speaking events and show edited versions. Don't become a "talking head" that joins all the rest of the bobble-heads. Many top speakers today don't even create "demo videos" anymore for bureaus and prospects, instead directing potential bookers and buyers to their websites and their streaming media. If you have a great voice, create weekly podcasts. Even at five minutes each, people can download them and listen in their cars or while walking down the block.

  Just because video is available, don't use it! The amateurish "welcome to my site" stuff is a quick turn-off that screams, "I can't afford to do this well, but I'm going to do it anyway."

- *Talk to me.* Don't read to me, and don't make me read. For one thing, talk to a camera as if you're having a conversation with it (e.g., with one person, not orating to an audience). Second, don't fill all that important website real estate with weak and boring text.

  Use enthusiasm and energy, which tend to be infectious. If you can't come across that way, then either you need some coaching or you need better ideas! Try a case study, where you present a challenge, and use both video and effects to help resolve it using your approaches.

- *Take either side of an interview.* Have someone off- or on-camera interview you, but in a non-infomercial manner, so that you're delving into detail about challenges, priorities, client successes, and so on. Or, interview a client, on camera, in terms of what your partnership created for their organization and for them, personally.

  These are better short than long, with many rather than a few. So a dozen one-minute interviews are far superior to one 12-minute interview.

- *Go viral.* It's usually easier than you think, but it's not as easy as some would wish. Publish content weekly on YouTube, Vimeo, Viddler, AudioAcrobat, iTunes, Blog Talk Radio, and a myriad of others.[4]

  You can leverage search engines such as Google to index your content, making it that much easier for others to locate and use. You can also replicate it with links and notations on social media platforms. This kind of ongoing repurposing creates true viral marketing since nothing is ever "lost," and the more your name is used, the more searches will turn up all of your content, not merely current content.

- *Step out in the crowd.* We've both created "100 Tips for _____" (fill in the blank). They go up daily (you can build your "bank" of these ahead of time) on various platforms and sites. You can gather them all and publish an ebook of your best work (*The Best of Jordan Adams on the Web*).

What can you do that will be a compelling and continual reason for people to seek you out?Here is an example of Alan's current content production on the internet:

- *Balancing Act®*: monthly newsletter on life balance
- *Million Dollar Consulting® Mindset*: monthly newsletter on consulting
- *Alan's Monday Morning Memo®*: weekly quick notes on success.
- *Friday Funnies*: weekly blog post featuring Alan's dogs
- *Writing on the Wall*: monthly video series on professional growth
- *Mentor Newsletter*: monthly newsletter for mentor participants
- *Workshop News*: monthly announcements on new opportunities

---

[4] There is no way to keep a book up to date on the latest of such devices, so visit our online Appendix, or do a simple Google search, as new alternatives are constantly appearing.

- *Alan's Friday Wrap™*: weekly podcasts and monthly videos on business
- *AlansForums.com*: chat room where Alan posts daily; monthly new articles
- *Alan's Blog*: new text, audio, and video on average three times weekly

This doesn't count assorted articles and interviews that Alan is involved with for third parties.

Virtual Reality

Ironically, the web is underutilized for professional promotion, or social media platforms are mistaken for promotion. Step out from the crowd.

When you put this book down after this particular reading, immediately jot down three new things you can do on the internet that involve spreading your value and worth using the web's unique abilities to help you.

One key is to be nimble and fast. Even with the staggering numbers on the internet, those who get there "firstest with the moistest" (to quote Confederate General Nathan Bedford Forrest) will be the most recognized. Your phrases, trademarks, copyrighted material, ideas, intellectual property, and so forth will be acknowledged as the source *if you take pains to ensure that you create a lot of it, spread it around to maximum effect with maximum delivery vehicles, and are clear about the credit being yours.*

If you're successful in this approach, you'll begin to create change that will grow in astounding increments. But you start with one step at a time.

3

Changing the World One Community at a Time

large progress in small increments

💲 Virtual communities produce very real profits

There are profits and there are profits. When developing global virtual communities, one has to think in terms of:

- finance
- personal
- spiritual
- short and long term
- business development
- social
- intellectual
- virtual and real

What draws people to communities is subject to a great deal of (mostly nonsensical) debate. For example, it isn't, in our experience, about low price or chat rooms or high tech, *per se*. There are, rather, three key elements:

1. *The inherent value derived from being there.* This must be manifest and unmistakable.

2. *The other people who are there.* Is there a developmental and ego need being met through peers?

3. *The virtual environment.* Is it friendly, easy to enter, readily available, simple to navigate, and so on?

These elements, in turn, are functions of your brand. If your brand, and the trust it implies, is strong, you can create instant credibility, draw people who are highly attractive to others, and acquire the talents required to create great technology (and gain the benefit of the doubt when the inevitable glitches occur, no small consideration and advantage).

Communities can be macro or micro, stand-alone or under other umbrellas. They will strengthen your brand in a wonderful reciprocity, as your brand strengthens the community. The magic is to ensure that they are perceived as building your clients' success and brands, and not just your own.

For example, AlansForums.com provides a variety of boards and threads in which members can share triumphs (and gain plaudits from peers) and reveal setbacks candidly or anonymously (and receive guidance from peers), all under the monitoring of our expertise. About 80 percent of the issues are self-sanctioned, but we have to step in at times to squelch some atrocious advice or add some wisdom. Hence, AlansForums is considered not only a safe place, but a springboard to build business rapidly from highly relevant and empathic colleagues.

The primary utility of DVRs and various video recorders is that they time-shift programming and remove commercial interruption. That's why standard commercial support for TV will eventually have to change, and we're already seeing it in extensive product placement (all those Coke glasses in front of *American Idol* judges) and entire programs sponsored by a single entity whose name is attached to the event.

Internet communities will continue to serve an analogous purpose: They provide for the time-shifting on a 24/7 basis of expertise from around the world, so that people from Australia, Chile, Canada, Italy, and the Philippines can all comment and reply within relatively brief time spans to each other. Second, they eliminate the noise of the internet. The claim of social media platforms is that they "amplify" messages. Perhaps, but just as when everything is a priority, nothing is a priority, when everything is amplified there is just a cacophony, not a perceived message.

Virtual communities, therefore, are highly valuable in time-shifting and providing focused amplification. The community is constantly communicating and improving itself, even as ant colonies and beehives must eventually rest.

And then there is the "water cooler" effect.

As you can see in Figure 3.1, all organizations have "water cooler talk" (aka "The Grapevine"), and the question is whether the energies of the participants are focused on customers or internal issues. The danger of virtual communities is that people simply remain in them and never meet customers or prospects. They pontificate on philosophy from their aeries but never get into the trenches, where the rough and tough sinners are running the world.

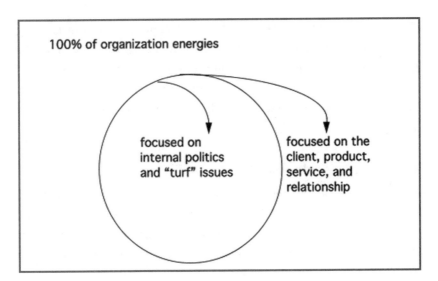

Figure 3.1: **Where is the energy going?**

Hence, outstanding communities allow for the water-cooler talk but are also effectively self-sanctioning in that they demand evidence and examples to back up opinions. For us, social media platforms such as Facebook are little more than water cooler communities, absorbing perhaps 85 percent of the energy invested, and tend to become quite addictive. Virtual communities must serve personal and professional objectives far better than the equivalent of pixilated crack cocaine.

Virtual Reality

We create and favor communities that provide a return on investment and don't simply consume discretionary time. You might call this "ROC," return on community.

Let's explore the very real profits (ROC) that virtual communities can produce.

The ultimate lab

The exchange of ideas, intellectual property, and initiatives in a *trusting* community can accelerate progress by focusing the best and the brightest on the issues. Virtual communities can be a "skunk works" of research and development for entrepreneurs, solo practitioners, boutique firm owners, and others who lack personal resources to hone and refine major plans.

New product and service generation

We've launched, as a direct result of community feedback and organic support, workshops, coaching, and consulting based on strategy, coaching, workshop creation, thought leadership, new product development, and many more. These offerings have exceeded a million dollars of revenue over just two years, with a built-in generation from potential participants and immediate support from a critical mass of registrants. The "Best Practices" workshop drew 110 people at $1,000 each the first time it was run (it's since been run in London and Sydney), and "Six Figures to Seven" drew a total of 70 people on three continents at $5,000 apiece.

Decrease expense

No one who can type and read need ever reinvent a wheel in virtual communities. The product or service, its origins and online citations and examples are quickly found. This decreases costs and reduces time in development, while also preventing following a path already trod or perfecting something already in use and proprietary.

In summary, learning is accelerated in these communities in the same way a particle accelerator speeds up matter, but without the violent crash! Questions can be answered in minutes, knowledge gained in an instant, and ideas solicited continually. It's a key spoke in the market gravity wheel and prompts the fulfillment of the accelerant curve.

And not incidentally, true communities create lifelong partnerships, collegiality, and even friendships, no small feat in a lone-wolf profession and increasingly impersonal world.

Showing up

For the true, web-based, virtual community there is a prime directive: People have to show up.

In working with insurance companies, we had to explain that they could prosper without agents so long as there were people needing insurance, but they could not prosper without prospective insurance customers even if they had ten thousand agents. Insurers kept getting their customers mixed up.

Similarly, all the technology in the world, whether it be holographic imaging or mind melds (a staple of Vulcan communities) will be useless without the "room" being occupied by interesting people who represent valuable relationships to others.

So what are the secrets?

Ten tips for thriving virtual communities

1. *You unlock the place and turn on the lights,* then make sure it's unlocked and lighted several times a day. The host and the moderator (if different people) must show up regularly and manifest their presence especially at the outset. This can be abetted by indicators showing who's been present over the past 15 minutes, or hour, or half-day. That way people will know you're around even if you're not currently posting or not online at the moment.

2. *They won't come just because you build it.* This isn't *Field of Dreams.* You have to promote your community aggressively. Our recommendations:

   - Your blog
   - Your mailing lists
   - Incentive offers
   - Professional associations
   - Others' blogs (reciprocate)
   - Social media platforms
   - Excerpts from postings
   - Citing it in your activities

3. *Encourage a meritocracy.* The worst communities in terms of longevity and attraction are those where anyone can post a comment and it receives immediate validity *through the mere act of posting.* Not all suggestions are good (or ethical or legal), and you must be prepared to provide feedback ranging from support, to correction, to critique, to slap-down. These communities are not democracies, they are benevolent dictatorships.

4. *Create rules.* There have to be clearly enforced guidelines about language (we're appalled at the obscenity on YouTube, for example, which cheapens the entire place unnecessarily), dealing with others, promotional activities, privacy, and so on. We also demand no smoking or cell phone use in our online communities.

5. *Provoke the hell out of people.* One editor published a column that people hated and wrote in to protest by the hundreds. He

immediately received an offer to write a column and commensurate payment. Why? Because he wasn't running a magazine to be loved, he was running one to be READ. People will come back if they are stimulated, not if they are bored. That's why 99.9 percent of the 200 million-plus global blogs are worthless—they are poorly written and, worse, boring.

6. *Play show tunes.* By that we mean, allow people to trumpet their triumphs. So long as they share their methodology and experiences so that others can profit, don't let your ego get in the way of others expounding upon their successes. You're supposed to provide a forum for the community, not a soap box for you. Encourage everyone to play their "greatest hits."

7. *Squelch the whining.* We believe that any "victimization" community should be nuked. (Well, at least infected with red ants.) You want to create a cycle of excitement and success, not commiseration in misery. (If you don't believe that exists, visit any Mensa meeting where people are forever crying that their "gifts" aren't "understood." If you're that smart, you should be able to hold a job successfully, period.)

Virtual Reality

Quality is more important than merely quantity in communities. That's because quantity can disappear, but quality will draw more people over time.

8. *Encourage sub-communities.* Think "web-like," no pun intended. (Well, maybe a small one.) You want people to get together offline in mastermind groups, or workshops, or other relationships. As you read this, sub-communities that call themselves "Alan's Groupies" are meeting in Australia; Ireland; the Pacific Northwest; New York; Washington, DC; and a host of other places.

9. *Throw the rascals out.* There will be times, albeit rarely, when members abuse their privileges by inappropriate language, or solicitation, or just general obnoxiousness. You have to have the volition (and technology) to deny them future entry after a warning or two. We've tossed four people over seven years. Good riddance. We have to keep the park clean and safe.

10. *Never forget that your value is virtual.* You are generating tremendous value through the mere existence of your community. You don't have to be present all the time or, eventually, even most of the time. But people will not forget that the value they derive originates with you, your brand, your creation. What you're creating is a legacy.

Communities are like solar systems. There are stars and planets, asteroids and meteors, quarks and neutrinos, suns and black holes. The cosmos overlaps, and so do communities. You can embrace other entire communities, or parts of them. You can create sub-systems, as we discussed above. You need to accept constantly moving, evolving, ambiguity. Once you try to create hard boundaries and fixed parameters, the communities will fracture as they attempt to migrate.

Ironically, in a world of "instant access" we are all feeling like lone wolves! That is, we communicate by screen and keyboard and text and video without another person next to us. We spend more time with screens than we do with books. No two screens are alike. We're more and more isolated and apart if we're not careful.

Communities can resolve that problem. There is a commonality and belonging that, while not quite a decoder ring or secret handshake (which we understand are still in use by quality teams), there is the epitome of the old refrain from the TV comedy *Cheers*: It's the place where they always know your name. A not-so-well-known parallel was penned by Robert Frost: "Home is the place where, when you go there, they have to take you in."

Community 601

We'll leave this subject for now with our "graduate-level" advice for sophisticated community creation and development.

- *Differentiate within the community.* Allow a variety of "boards" and subjects. You may want to assign moderators to varied boards, but they would have to have the same discipline and emotional investment that you do. For example, in the financial area, you could have one board on compliance, another on retirement, another on valuation, and still another on life balance. On AlansForums.com, people can ask for personal help anonymously.

- *Don't be afraid to create "elites."* We restrict some boards to people who have attended certain workshops or who have attained certain accolades (e.g, the Mentor Hall of Fame). So long as others have sufficient variety outside of these, they serve as an inducement to advance to further levels of the community. Make no mistake, once you're with the "in crowd," normative pressure creates the motivation to move to even "inner crowds."

- *Create shortcuts to eliminate noise or rise above the fray.* One can "Ask Alan" in the forum to receive a private reply. If anyone else comments, they're fined $10, payable to the local animal protection league. (We've collected a couple of hundred dollars.)

- *Either suggest or demand that all participants use real names and photos.* This is what creates true communities and inspires people to be polite, helpful, and present.

- *Never use the term "lurkers" or discourage them.* People who simply come to read and/or listen and learn are welcome in our communities. To demand that they post and contribute is akin to the Twitter lunacy that you're impolite if you don't follow those following you.

Now let's examine these "cosmos" more closely.

The nebula effect

A nebula is an interstellar cloud. The matter within them coalesces to form stars and other objects. That's because of an internal gravity that draws things closer and together. They can be vast or small, and often embrace and incorporate other nebulae.

We believe you can see where we're going with this.

Communities are analogous to nebulae. They gather people, many of whom exert a gravitational pull on others, who come together to form still tighter communities within the whole. They are constantly growing, expanding, moving. They can be observed from great distances. And they are concurrently porous—people come and go, there are varied barriers (or lack thereof) to entry—and hard, in that there is a commonality that self-excludes some and certain rules or laws that govern the dynamics.

We've found that viral marketing is the equivalent of the "black stuff" that scientists believe constitutes the great bulk of unseen matter in the universe. You can't often see viral marketing, but you can certainly experience the impact of its results.

When atomic energy was new, there were TV programs trying to explain how it worked. One, focusing on chain reactions, had a ping-pong table filled with mouse traps that were primed, each with a ping-pong ball on the mechanism. The narrator tossed a ball on to the table and, sure enough, the released balls triggered others until the entire table was a mass of hopping balls. It was a pretty good example for the layman, which we were.

The same principle holds true for our nebula effect and the power of viral marketing. Tossing one ball—one insightful bit of knowledge, or value, or experience, or appeal—can create an enormous chain reaction of promotion and marketing and prominence. This is one of the reasons that we advise everyone to turn their intellectual capital into intellectual property and get it into your communities. Stop worrying about people "stealing" it and start preparing for people using it successfully and coming to you for more—with money in their hands.

Within communities, you can break the laws of mathematics, because 1 + 1 can equal 86. Those are the ping-pong balls triggered by just a single toss onto the table.

Virtual Reality

The iPhone and iPad phenomena are not just about communications, the internet, or technology. They are about the reciprocating nature of communities, and the virtual perpetual-motion machine.

We create communities that should be able to perpetuate themselves, virtual perpetual-motion machines. How is this possible? Because of the principle of REV™: reciprocating, exponential value.

Exploring REV

With the introduction of the iPhone, Apple created a platform for developers to launch varied applications—"apps." Today, "there's an app for that" has entered the vernacular. Designers created (at this writing) over a quarter-million apps that attracted a huge amount of users, which encouraged Apple to continue to improve the iPhone through several versions and create the iPad, which in turn drew more users, which encouraged still more app designers. You get the picture.

REV is based on the premise that the more value a community produces and manifests,[1] the more it attracts valuable assets—people. And the more valuable people it will attract, the more other people, who desire to be with them, will also join. All of these folks will be creating value in addition to the value that you provide, so the chain reaction continues to grow.

---

[1] If it's not seen, it's not worth it.

And when people in the community derive value from being with each other, that value accrues to you, because you are the reason that the community exists.

Our "Private Roster Mentor Program" has spawned the "Mentor Hall of Fame" and "Master Mentor Programs." AlansForums.com has created a dozen workshop groups, scores of mastermind groups, and the regional meetings referred to above. The Million Dollar Club, Society for Advancement of Consulting, and other groups all overlap with these, some people belonging to all, some to just one; some groups requiring qualifications, some open to everyone; some costing money to join, some free. Community members are constantly talking to each other, comparing notes, and urging others to engage in more activities.

That's REV, the perpetual-motion machine running the nebula.

Some people will come and go, but as the community grows, the "core" grows, so that there is an increasingly stronger gravitational pull. The community organizer's role is to deliver the mail and protect the coasts (e.g., to insert value and to monitor for propriety). Our most successful communities actually create their own "best practices" and share them on their own volition.

The graphic in Figure 3.2 demonstrates REV. The area designated as

- C indicates the prime, or original community created by the entrepreneur.
- C2 represents the inner community within the prime community.
- C3 shows another existing community being embraced by members of the prime and inner communities.
- C4 indicates the fully-embraced new community, with C5.
- C5 delineates an elite community formed by membership in prime, C2, and C4 communities.
- C6 shows an existing community being drawn by the gravity of the growing prime community.

So long as you continue to import your own value to the communities, and to attract people who, in turn, provide high

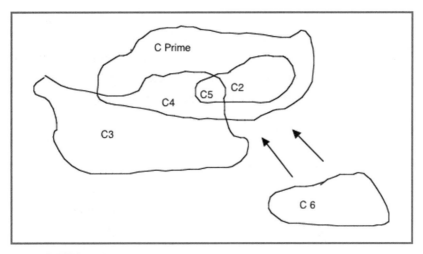

Figure 3.2: **REV in action**

perceived value, the communities will grow and morph. They will form sub-sections and elites, embrace newcomers, and exponentially enhance the gravity and attraction.

That viral marketing can be thus stimulated and augmented by utilizing social media platforms, workshops, speeches, publishing, newsletters, blogs, podcasts, teleconferences, and so on. Provide downloads for free (samples of those "best practices"). Consider subscription levels (silver, gold, platinum) which offer increasing exposure to intellectual property and opportunities. "Alan & The Gang," for example, offers responses to questions on a global basis for a charge per question, or for free at certain membership levels. The "Gang" comprises members of the inner community who volunteer for the positions in return for prominent publicity and links to their companies.

Ironically, virtual communities are most greatly enhanced by real-time meetings. This is why we encourage the sub-groups to meet, and why we fund and sponsor a "Mentor Summit" every nine months, so that people who are accustomed to interacting online can periodically interact in person. This hugely increases their community participation. People come from all over the world to these summits.

The nebula effect is different from the cosmos in that you control this, not the forces of nature. You need to talk in the plural—"communities"—but also to learn where to put the "stay off the grass" and "beware of dog" signs.

Fences and "beware of dog" signs

On a more down-to-earth basis, there are boundaries that shouldn't be ignored or violated. You need some rules to govern the place. Here are the rules for AlansForums.com, some more serious than others:

Forum rules, enforced by radar

- No inappropriate language or offensive tone.
- No personal attacks.
- No promotion of products or services.
- No refunds.
- No smoking.
- No cell phones.
- No plagiarism or theft of others' ideas.
- You can be removed unilaterally if these rules have been violated.
- Refer any technological problems to the *Forum Administrator*.
- Refer any comments about content or behavior to *The Doge*.

You want to avoid the chaos and anarchy found on places like Facebook and YouTube, while also allowing for the free expression of opinion and healthy disagreement.

It's difficult to determine members' success level, and some can fall into the trap of heeding advice of unsuccessful people. (Among the few people we've tossed off of our communities are those we *knew* to be unsuccessful and lying about their experiences to support bogus claims of successful techniques.) We keep emphasizing that there is no resident "faculty" to provide the "right" answers, and we sanction commentary that, even with the best of intentions, is, well, loony. The best community members listen and ask more than talk and answer.

Virtual Reality

Establish your fences and boundaries, and then let the dogs loose on the other side.

The good news is that most communities can be wondrously self-regulating. The power of the place—almost as in a huge focus group—to discipline members and peers who cross the line (jump the fence) is impressive. (There are your barking dogs.) We've had people in our forums who just wanted to argue with everyone, and probably would have fought physically if they could have. They belong in cage fighting communities, not ours.

Here are three of the cardinal sins to beware of and punish:

1. *Hijacking.* This occurs when a thread is stolen according to one's personal agenda. Example: Someone posts, "Customers can be obnoxious at times and aren't automatically right." Another responds, "I wasn't wrong when I complained to the phone company, and they had the nerve to delay my new system." That's a private agenda run amok.

2. *Self-promotion.* We find this frequently on our blogs, as well. Under the guise of a post, the writer notes, "Click on this for more information," and they are, of course, selling electric forks or "get rich marketing in social media" books. This is why moderation is vital. Delete these and make sure you have the technology to block the address in the future.

3. *Ego explosions.* There are people hell-bent on proving how smart they are who are, in reality, simply proving how rapidly they can consult Wikipedia (which, of course, had Senator Kennedy deceased while he was still very much alive). These folks need to

be dealt with offline and, if they don't stop, barred. (When we told one person that he had the habit of adding a personal story to everyone's comments, he actually responded, "You know, I had to deal with someone just like this when I taught classes at . . . ."!)

There are myriad techniques to create the positive, constructive, self-sanctioning community that represent low labor intensity for you but high value for community members.

One is to encourage the use of real names and real photos. Those icons and pictures of the family dog or baby girl are cutesy, but are really masks to hide behind. There is a direct correlation between responsible behavior and having to reveal one's identity and image. We mandate that real names and actual photos be used. It was fascinating that, once we did, the photos became far more professional and higher quality. Everyone wanted to look their best!

Another important technique is to encourage "veterans" to contribute and appear regularly. They create and convey the mores and norms of the community more frequently and effectively than the random interventions of the moderator and/or owners. We do this in various ways:

- Pop quizzes and tests that the veterans love to compete in.
- Case studies that are "answered" by the owner after at least 24 hours, giving people in all time zones the opportunity to contribute their responses.
- Live chats, where we are answering questions in real time and providing the chat as a download later for those who can't make the live event. These have drawn up to 25 percent of the community at any given time. (The technology has advanced from on-screen typing to live interaction.)
- Monthly articles posted solely on the forum and nowhere else, intended exclusively for members of the community.

You also must monitor spam registrations carefully, since the lowlifes accelerate their technology as fast as anyone. Under no circumstances do you want privacy violated, and you should notify anyone who appears to be contacting other community members to promote products, "multi-level marketing" (Ponzi schemes), and involvement of third parties that such activity is unwarranted.

Foster powerful content from yourself and your members. Think of this as a private party (not a flea market or bar) where everyone has a good time and drinks responsibly. Just as you wouldn't allow a rude guest in your home, but would embrace those who are the "life of the party," the same attitude should obtain for your virtual communities. No one should say something online that they wouldn't say in person.

We have small fines ($10) for various infractions, which we send to charity. That keeps a soft, humorous, but constant reminder in place that minor transgressions will be dealt with so that they don't become larger transgressions.

Unlike most communities, you can create yours from scratch and determine who joins it. Let's turn now to how you use that tailored community to build your brand and your repute.

Branding by Bonding

ensuring that they just can't get enough of you

Beating your own drum

Your brands should be memorable, not time-related to an event, compelling, and carry implied value. Complete the following sentence when an interviewer says, "Tell me who you are":

I am _____.

A brand is a representation of uniform value that most often creates both intellectual attraction and, more important, emotional appeal and even cachet. Most people you ask will tell you that Coca Cola or Coke is the strongest brand in the world followed closely by McDonald's. A few years ago, *Business Week*, which uses a formula to calculate brand value (not the worth of the company, but the worth of the brand appeal in building business) placed Coke on top of the list, at $80 billion.

But at this writing, and for the past two years, the brand king has been Google. The web builds brands at the speed of light.

So if you believe, as we do, that logic makes people think, but emotion makes them act, ask yourself these questions when people consider your brand or brands:

· Is it something special?
· What kind of emotions do you want to generate?
· Are you someone with whom they would like to do business or follow?

Trust, innovation, quality, and growth

"If you don't blow your own horn, there is no music." At some point your horn can become a full orchestra, augmented by the power of the leverage and scalability of the web, under your "baton." The key is to create this presence in a non-narcissistic way, looking like a valued asset and not a late-night infomercial.

The strongest brand is your name. "Get me Joan Larson" is a far better dynamic than "Get me an excellent strategist" and Joan happens to be a possible name among many. Not many people have said, "We need Summit Consulting Group." They say, "We need Alan Weiss."

But on the way to your name recognition, and often in conjunction with your name recognition, you can and should create brands that "play well" on the web and enhance your appeal (Alan is also known widely as The Contrarian, The Rock Star of Consulting, and as The Million Dollar Consultant, for example). We've helped people develop:

· The Lion Tamer (working with aberrant behavior in executives)
· Lifeblood (working in the biotech field)
· The Technology Tailor
· The Performance Architect
· The Sales Accelerator

Your brands should be memorable, not time-related to an event, compelling, and carry implied value. Try again to complete the following sentence when an interviewer says, "Tell me who you are":

I am _____.

Search your brands and the ones of your colleagues and competitors. For example: YouTube www.youtube.com or the advanced search tools of Google www.google.com/advanced_search or Twitter http://search.twitter.com/advanced, or set up automatic alerts through Google Alerts www.google.com/alerts or subscribe to automatically receive important blogs updates using Google Reader www.google.com/reader. When searching your name, company name, and brands that are associated with you, what do you see? Are the results vast, impressive, and complementing your credibility, or not?

Find out for yourself if people are being exposed to a coherent, clear "story" about your value, or if they find a gallimaufry of odd notices and references.

If you do find that your brand is not consistently expressed or strong, try these techniques:

- Position yourself as the brand while publishing. For example: "Chad's 10 SEO Myths" or "Alan's 101 Sales Question for Every Sales Situation."
- Publish often, which means several times a week on your blog and at least monthly articles on your site, contribute your expertise to online communities and social media, and provoke with questions.
- Engage and build online relationships with thought leaders and influential bloggers. Consider the following:

  - Comment on their sites, blogs, and social media profiles with provocative yet helpful content.
  - Mention their content, products, and services in your content such as articles, podcasts, and videos.

- Suggest additional resources.
- Interview them.
- Offer to be interviewed.
- Monitor what is being said about you and your brand and interact quickly with both the good and the bad. (Dave Carroll, www. davecarrollmusic.com, while travelling on United Airlines, broke his guitar. The difference was astounding between United's poor reaction to the viral video Dave created vs. the creative reaction of Bob Taylor, the CEO of the guitar manufacturer, offering a free guitar!)
- Connect with journalists and provide them with relevant and interesting information for their followers.

How many of these activities are you engaged in? We'll bet too few. (One of the best ways to promote your brand is through community building, and we've devoted an entire chapter to that pursuit.)

Virtual Reality

Use your brand or brands consistently, attaching them to every possible opportunity. You must continually "play" your message.

Learn from the best and emulate their approaches. Who appeals to you, and why? Whose brands are easiest for you to remember and use when you make purchasing decisions? We think you'll see the following commonalities:

- Attractive design around the brand
- Utilized in books
- Podcasts on the site, blog, and iTunes
- Videos on the site, blog, and YouTube
- Huge supporting content and value
- Workshops, teleconferences, webinars

CASE STUDY
Developing a Website

My first web step was to develop a blog with frequent provocative postings, guest articles, and a customized look and feel that began to generate interesting comments and gained awards for the posts. I used the material as the basis for a regular newsletter. Stimulating conversations were going on with people in different parts of the world. These conversations were about ideas and philosophies about organizational change, and I was being seen as a leader. However, they weren't telling potential customers what I could do for them, and they didn't have a customer voice saying what I'd done for them.

I then learned that a website is a credibility statement to support my prospects in deciding to work with me as a consultant. So I decided to create a website to support the potential client's process of engaging with me as their consultant. A number of web providers I talked to didn't understand this, and I needed a website that helped me gain new clients.

That's why I engaged Chad Barr, who developed a website that showcased my value proposition and that gave prominence to customer testimonials. This has changed my interactions with potential clients. When referrals contact me (and they have all been referred by someone else) they have looked up my site and seen what clients say about me. Personally, I think the best thing is having the testimonials rotate on the front page. The most important thing for me is that when I am contacted by potential clients, they have checked out the website and they have seen what clients say about me. They ask, "How can we work together?" not "What are your credentials?" Not long after my website went live, I got my first international coaching client, from the website, and we used Skype to communicate. I had to worry about how to accept international payments. Not a bad problem to have!

—Stephen Billing, Director, Exponential Consulting, Ltd.
www.exponentialconsulting.com
Reprinted with permission of Stephen Billing ©2011. All rights reserved.

- Speaking engagements
- Constant reinvention and evolution

The unmined ore of your brand reach is probably your own database. Once you interact with someone, be sure to consider:

- After initial purchase, use an autoresponder to thank them and offer additional value and offerings.
- Various newsletters containing how-to content, interviews as well as incentives.
- Promotion newsletter with special offers and announcements.
- Increase the size and quality of your database by creating landing pages that offer enticements to the visitor for providing their email address. Alan routinely sends out gifts to every 500th new follower on Twitter, for example.

The turbo charge to building powerful brands is to provide value to your clients, prospects, and visitors that generates results that demonstrably improve their condition.

Viral branding

Our definition of viral branding, pragmatically, is: the creation of excitement ("buzz," "jazz," aggressive word-of-mouth) that is contagious and infectious. It influences individuals to share and excite other individuals about your content, products, services, and mere presence.

Viral branding creates *internet evangelists*. The power is exponential.

The best way to create viral branding—where people are taking up your causes and informing others, especially on massive platforms such as those of social media—is to develop and promote outstanding ideas, concepts, and offerings that will cause others to feel they will be well-regarded by those they advise to access them. These fans or evangelists are online advocates.

Seth Godin, the noted author and speaker (*The Purple Cow, Tribes*) creates this kind of viral effect. Another example is our own community, AlansForums.com, which has attracted a thousand consultants globally and drawn 80,000 posts, as well as generated its own MasterMind groups, teleconferences, consulting models, and so

Figure 4.1: **Viral bundling on Amazon.com**

forth. People feel they are doing others a favor by referring them to Seth's or our sites.

Publishing is a key to brand strength and viral acceleration. Others are doing the work for you. Figure 4.1 shows how Amazon.com spreads the news and promotes your books and your works to others on a continuing basis.

You learn of new books, related older books, and can access the author's own pages on Amazon.

Assertively approach your friends, colleagues, partners, staff, associates, and others (especially your customers or clients) to help you spread the word. Most will gladly help, many because they realize you will reciprocate one day, or they are reciprocating for your past help to them.

You can provide for this on your blog or in your newsletter. In Figure 4.2, you see Alex Goldfayn on Facebook promoting his evangelist marketing. There is huge leverage and scalability available on social media platforms. Many people simply want to be a part of an exciting offering, without any particular *quid pro quo*. You can augment this with viral products such as ebooks in PDF formats that you encourage others to share. (At this writing, Seth Godin has decided to bypass conventional publishers altogether and simply publish directly on the web.)

Don't be obsessesed with protection. Make it excessively easy for your fans to share your work and intellectual property with others. For the past several years we've used WordPress as a platform and our main development engine in coding clients' websites. While enabling design freedom, we can also create functionally rich and sophisticated sites while implementing powerful, third-party plug-ins (stand-alone software functionality), or our own. We can readily include social media clickable links and allow visitors to share those pages with others. *We want visitors to be able to easily spread the word by showing the goods!*

When posting audio (say, podcast MP3 format) files on your site and blog, be sure to integrate it with iTunes. This will propagate your content by leveraging one of the largest and most amazing repositories, which Apple is providing for your use. This allows individuals to search and explore and to locate your content, independent of your own sites, and allows them to be immediately redirected to your sites.

Figure 4.2: **A master of viral branding**
Reprinted with permission of Alex Goldfayn ©2011. All rights reserved.

Publishing your videos on platforms such as YouTube (probably the largest "social media" site) provides the same potential for video. The titles and tags you can assign will ensure your video turns up in the right searches and grabs attention. Others can actually embed your material in their sites to further spread the word dramatically.

Virtual Reality

Stop being obsessed with protection of your work, and start being consumed by the viral dissemination of your work. Lawsuits are not profit centers.

You need to actually reduce the restriction for access, which is counterintuitive for most people, but makes absolute sense on the web and in viral marketing. Some examples of successful viral branding:

- Hotmail and Gmail, which are free email programs offered by Microsoft and Google, respectively.
- Our client, Bill Zipp, has provided free access to many of his articles, worksheets, and process visuals and selective access to other resources (see Figure 4.3).
- Groupon's deal-of-the-day website to promote and provide local offerings to consumers (www.groupon.com).
- The Grateful Dead (www.dead.net) provides free music downloads to entice fans to attend concerts and purchase other products.
- The "Elf Yourself" holiday campaign provided by Office Max.
- Firefox as an open-source browser.
- Wikipedia—the free encyclopedia.
- Social media sites such as Facebook, Twitter, and LinkedIn providing their platforms for free.
- The Apple app store with thousands of free apps.
- Anthony Robbins leveraging old media, new media, and affiliates.

Creating a "sticky" web presence

Many people spend their resources and energy trying to attract visitors to their sites. That seems reasonable and achievable. However, there are two aspects to "site power" that often defeat site owners who are investing heavily to attract visitors. In fact, we have a word for it: retention.

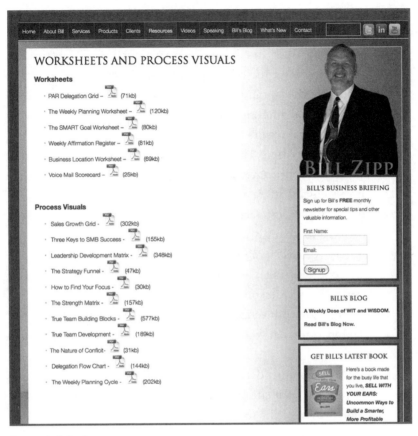

Figure 4.3: **Selective access**
Reprinted with permission of Bill Zipp ©2011. All rights reserved.

It's insufficient to merely attract people; you need to retain them. Not for hours or days, but for minutes and for repeat visits. We call this a "sticky" web presence, because people don't want to leave (and, yes, we make it difficult for them to leave—to get rid of us—because we're offering so much value, so many options, so much interest).

Here are different types of "sticky keys":

❏ Your site must be responsive and quick to load and display pages, otherwise visitors will quickly grow impatient and leave.

We once saw a site owner's "floating head," which took over a minute to make its message and clear the screen!

❑ Interesting, fresh and dynamic content, such as diagnostics and self-scoring tests and challenges for the visitor.

❑ Make sure the landing page answers what they came there to do with minimal amount of clicks or clutter. In other words, what are the typical results for the client or customer?

❑ Reduce stagnation. Three strikes and you are out. Keep it fresh and review your content for timeliness and relevance. If there are three things that are dated, the visitor is probably out.

❑ Enable visitor interaction though email, contact forms, comments, and sharing with others. Don't play hide-and-seek, or protect yourself more from prospects than you do from spam. For goodness' sake, list your physical address in case someone wants to mail you something![1]

❑ Community connections with peers and successful colleagues. Demonstrate that you're connected to the industry and the community.

❑ Others' recommendations. Include video and print testimonials throughout your site, not merely on a "testimonial page."

❑ Ability to subscribe to newsletters, email notification alerts, and RSS feeds. Allow people to gain continuous access via other platforms.

❑ Create incentives such as: "You will receive instantly . . ." Let people download text, audio, and video.

❑ Promote your best content with "The Best of . . ." articles. This can often be a list of Twitter posts you've made on common subjects, recycling and repurposing your intellectual property in new ways.

---

[1] Post office boxes don't hide your location, since, by law, any corporate postal box will have the owner's address revealed upon an inquiry to the postmaster. And if someone really wants to stalk and kill you, they don't need your website to find you.

- ❑ Show them additional resources on each page and what other visitors have liked. Amazon is great for this: "Others who read this book have also purchased . . . ."
- ❑ When people leave comments, respond as quickly as possible and also thank them for stopping by and for their feedback. No inquiry should go unanswered for more than 24 hours.
- ❑ Create a continuing series (sequels) that builds on interest, suspense, and more intense future knowledge, such as Episode #1, #2, #3, or Part 1 of 3.
- ❑ Repurpose older content by adding new life to it. Include videos, or graphics, or case studies of how you've since applied it.
- ❑ Easy way to access the latest announcements, what's new, and upcoming events. The web page's margin real estate is quite effective for this.
- ❑ Upsell products and services during the checkout process by offering related items and other bundles. This is like the checkout line at your local Staples or Best Buy, with all kinds of impulse items for sale as you stand on line.

Customer engagement and relationship building should continue long after a site or non-site purchase. We capture every single book, video, audio, workshop, and related buyer's purchase and we email to them once a month. These ongoing updates of recent developmental experiences is one of our most effective and successful methods (see Figure 4.4 on page 80).

One of the slippery-slope, stickiness removers, is overly complex design and difficult navigation. Also, too many "orphan" pages, which require no action at all and go nowhere, tend to turn visitors toward the door. Make sure the visitor is compelled to do *something*. But keep it local. We generally use no links directing the buyer elsewhere (to another site). We want our sites to be cul-de-sacs where the buyer can stay put.

Developmental Experiences with Alan Weiss

Alan Weiss <Alan@SummitConsulting.com>

To: Chad Barr <chad@cbsoftware.com>

Some exciting things coming up:

THE TIME OF YOUR LIFE
May 10, The Platinum Hotel, Las Vegas, NV
http://summitconsulting.com/seminars/the-time-of-your-life-practicum.php

Learn how to plan your day, your week, your month, your year. Gain a month of discretionary time by learning Alan's techniques and approaches to organization, priorities, interruptions, technology, and leverage. One day that can gain you 30.

THE ODD COUPLE®
June 25-26, The Platinum Hotel, Las Vegas, NV
http://fripp.com/oddcouple.html

Join Alan and Patricia Fripp for a rollicking great time while learning these two experts' secrets of marketing for professional speakers. Over a decade of great fun and learning.

ALAN WEISS IN SYDNEY
November 16-17, Sydney, Australia
http://summitconsulting.com/seminars/alan-weiss-the-consultants-consultant-in-sydney.php

A "mini-Consulting College, with a quarter century of consulting success presented in terms of thought leadership, Million Dollar Referrals, exploiting the two sales you make with a proposal, remote coaching and consulting, setting the highest fees of your life and getting them before the project begins, and much more. First 25 people get a free, third morning with a personal debrief by Alan. Dinner for 12 available with Alan on November 15 (two seats remain!). The one-time opportunity of a lifetime.

MILLION DOLLAR CONSULTING® COLLEGE
May 23-27, and October 31-November 4, Castle Hill Inn, Newport, RI
http://summitconsulting.com/consulting-college/consulting_college_2011-05.php
http://summitconsulting.com/consulting-college/consulting_college_2011-09.php

Participate in the finest development anywhere for consultants and related professionals. Visit the pages above for testimonials and photos. Join 200 elite consultants worldwide who have participated.

OCEAN'S 11
June 23, 2011, MGM Lofts, Las Vegas, NV
bentleygtc@summitconsulting.com

Join Alan and a maximum of 10 other people to talk about business, philosophy, sex, religion, politics"whatever subjects come up in an 1800-square-foot, bi-level suite with 25-foot panoramic windows. Breakfast, lunch, breaks, and cocktails are all included. Consider this a professional and personal intellectual spa day. Only $1100. Four seats are filled, seven remain"you must email Alan directly for your place.

Figure 4.4: **Compelling the visitor to act**

Provide areas that invite response, such as: "We'd love to have your feedback, please click here." Ensure that your site is compatible with all major browsers, including Firefox, internet Explorer, Safari, and Chrome. No less than American Express has admitted that one of their merchant financial downloads won't work well with Safari! That's just lazy; there is no technological reason for it.

Make a list on the following lines of the "sticky" features on your site, or indicate those you'd like to immediately add:

____

_____

_____

_____

_____

_____

_____

_____

_____

_____

_____

_____

_____

_____

_____

_____

_____

_____

_____

_____

_____

Removing the
Immigration Agents

moving swiftly through borders
and boundaries

The global website

Noam Chomsky labels globalization as "international integration."
Thomas Friedman cites global economics as a leveled or flattened
playing field.

Some people cite "global" as beginning when people first looked
up at the stars, just as many see the current web as an extension of
Gutenberg's movable type. We tend to toss off the phrase easily and
with a tacit "wink" that we all know we live in "global times."

But what times are these, really?

From Columbus to the early 19th century, "globalization"
probably was represented by people walking aboard sailing ships and
pointing them toward the horizon, often as not finding something
they hadn't intended when they set out. Subsequent to that, it was
a capitalistic movement, with companies searching for both raw

materials and raw customers. The East India Company is an example of that kind of global business financed by an empire and later represented by Standard Oil or the United Fruit Company, financed by investors and propelled by avaricious commerce. ("Behind every great fortune is a great crime," observed Balzac.)

For at least the past decade, however, we're in a third phase, each one ever shorter, with globalization's propulsion provided by the individual over the web.

It took Moses 40 years to reach Canaan, and Columbus months to reach North America (which, as indicated, wasn't intended), and TWA days to get people cross-country by plane in the early '50s, prior to jets. Today, with the potential of the internet and power of a personal computer, one can build a global brand, business, community, and income within days. The digital empire isn't based on slow ships laden with silver and gold sailing through storms and pirates. It's about exploring, reaching, accelerating, and "conquering" *while reducing travel, overcoming language barriers, and overwhelming borders.*

Unlike Cortés, you don't have to burn the ships to force the troops to stay. There are no ships, no troops, and no reason to stay (or even visit).

Virtual Reality

It is quicker and easier to set up an international business site than it is to establish a physical business in your local town.

In 2011 alone, the "Arab spring" was fueled by internet communications. As evidence of the powerful nature of that community, Iran has tried to ban international internet access, which will probably be impossible to maintain. This community power enables people to rally, incite, evangelize, convert, influence, motivate, and discourage. Moreover, the combination of "legitimate" and "informal" global communications helps to legitimize all.

Journalists report from the field, embedded with troops or dodging tornados, in real time. A Pakistani man on Twitter noted the helicopters over his head as the U.S. Navy SEALs team stormed the Bin Laden complex and was soon deluged with thousands of tweets a minute asking for updates, to the extent that the system temporarily collapsed. How is he different from a journalist on site? Who is more interesting to communicate with? You can't question the journalist. Who is more of a peer, likely to share your views? Not the journalist.

When we combine people, technology, and these new individual connections, we find in our hands an awesome power. The instantaneous, ubiquitous, omnipresent (but not omniscient) access enables people to immediately learn, react, make decisions, and create. What does this really mean for us and our businesses? No one in the time of Moses or Columbus or Juan Tripp at TWA was in as educated and pragmatic a position to make these determinations and analyses of this global power before us.

When we refer to the "global website," we are also embracing a global presence and global exposure. By the mere dint of launching your site, you are seen worldwide, or at least have that potential. That also creates our ongoing admonition about recognition: It's great to stand out in a crowd *so long as you look good while you're standing there*. Unfortunately, the majority of prospects we come across tend to think far too small, using a microscope, not a telescope, for their global strategy.

A year ago we estimated the number of internet users at almost 2 billion, which is about one in three people on earth, in jungles, deserts, mountaintops, and islands. You can see, in Figure 5.1 on page 86, that usage by language. (Note English and Chinese!) According to this site, www.internetworldstats.com/stats7.htm, over half a billion are English-speaking. Yet when you look at Figure 5.2, page 87, you'll also see the amazing potential of exploiting the use of other languages.

A great deal of the English usage can probably be attributed to the origins of the technology and ubiquitous nature of English in international affairs (e.g., air traffic control), but there's no guarantee that will continue.

INTERNET WORLD USERS BY LANGUAGE
Top 10 Languages

Internet World Stats presents its latest estimates for Internet Users by Language Because of the importance of this research, and due to the lack of other sources, Internet World Stats publishes several tables and charts featuring analysis and details here below for the **top ten languages** and also for the detailed world languages in use by country.

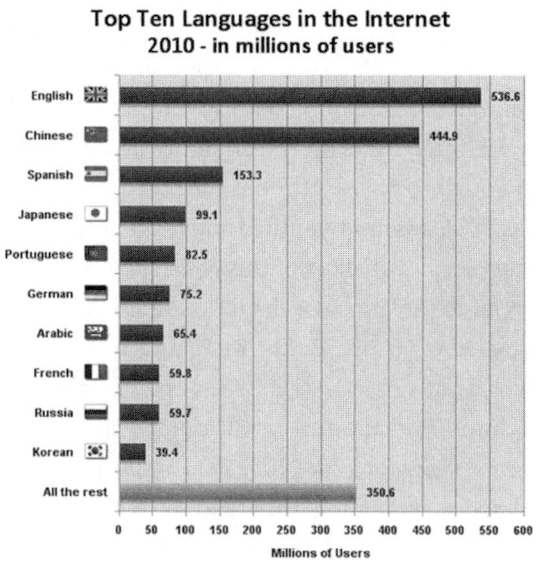

Top Ten Languages in the Internet
2010 - in millions of users

Language	Millions of Users
English	536.6
Chinese	444.9
Spanish	153.3
Japanese	99.1
Portuguese	82.5
German	75.2
Arabic	65.4
French	59.8
Russia	59.7
Korean	39.4
All the rest	350.6

Source: Internet World Stats - www.internetworldstats.com/stats7.htm
Estimated Internet users are 1,966,514,816 on June 30, 2010
Copyright © 2000 - 2010, Miniwatts Marketing Group

Figure 5.1: **Top languages on the internet**
Reprinted with permission of Enrique De Argaez ©2011. All rights reserved.

Are you promoting your global brand at the moment, and if so, to what degree of efficacy? Are you giving serious consideration to languages other than English?

There are times when it's clearly advantageous to promote other languages on your own site. Three primary options exist:

Top Ten Languages Used in the Web
(Number of Internet Users by Language)

TOP TEN LANGUAGES IN THE INTERNET	Internet Users by Language	Internet Penetration by Language	Growth in Internet (2000 - 2010)	Internet Users % of Total	World Population for this Language (2010 Estimate)
English	536,564,837	42.0 %	281.2 %	27.3 %	1,277,528,133
Chinese	444,948,013	32.6 %	1,277.4 %	22.6 %	1,365,524,982
Spanish	153,309,074	36.5 %	743.2 %	7.8 %	420,469,703
Japanese	99,143,700	78.2 %	110.6 %	5.0 %	126,804,433
Portuguese	82,548,200	33.0 %	989.6 %	4.2 %	250,372,925
German	75,158,584	78.6 %	173.1 %	3.8 %	95,637,049
Arabic	65,365,400	18.8 %	2,501.2 %	3.3 %	347,002,991
French	59,779,525	17.2 %	398.2 %	3.0 %	347,932,305
Russian	59,700,000	42.8 %	1,825.8 %	3.0 %	139,390,205
Korean	39,440,000	55.2 %	107.1 %	2.0 %	71,393,343
TOP 10 LANGUAGES	1,615,957,333	36.4 %	421.2 %	82.2 %	4,442,056,069
Rest of the Languages	350,557,483	14.6 %	588.5 %	17.8 %	2,403,553,891
WORLD TOTAL	1,966,514,816	28.7 %	444.8 %	100.0 %	6,845,609,960

(*) NOTES: (1) Top Ten Languages Internet Stats were updated for June 30 2010. (2) Internet Penetration is the ratio between the sum of Internet users speaking a language and the total population estimate that speaks that specific language. (3) The most recent Internet usage information comes from data published by Nielsen Online, International Telecommunications Union, GfK, and other reliable sources. (4) World population information comes from the U.S. Census Bureau . (5) For definitions and navigation help in several languages, see the Site Surfing Guide. (6) Stats may be cited, stating the source and establishing an active link back to Internet World Stats. Copyright © 2010, Miniwatts Marketing Group. All rights reserved worldwide.

Examples for interpretation of the data:
- There are **99,143,700** Japanese speaking people using the Internet, this represents **5.0 %** of all the Internet users in the world.
- Out of the estimated **126,804,433** population of the world that speaks Japanese, **78.2 %** use the Internet.
- The number of Japanese Speaking Internet Users has grown **110.6 %** in the last ten years (2000-2010).

Figure 5.2: **Specific language uses on the web**
Reprinted with permission of Enrique De Argaez ©2011. All rights reserved.

1. Keep your site in English and allow the visitor to use tools such as Google Translator to dynamically translate each page. This minimizes the labor necessary on your end but may create some inaccuracies in the automatic translation.
2. Various tools are available to automatically translate your site to predetermine languages that you would want to provide.
3. Professionally translate and have your site coded to support the desired languages. Figure 5.3 on page 88 shows www.stevesavage. com, which allows visitors to view the site in both English and Spanish (by clicking a link next to the search box in the upper right corner). In this example, the entire site has been carefully translated from English (primary audience) to Spanish (secondary audience) and coded to fully support both languages including multi-language use of videos. Yet in another example, in Figure

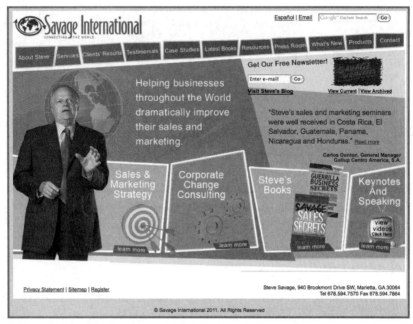

Figure 5.3: **A site offering two languages: English and Spanish**
Reprinted with permission of Steve Savage ©2011. All rights reserved.

5.4, www.mandat.de demonstrates the primary audience being German-speaking and the secondary audience, English-speaking.

 ## The global services provider

Why go global at all? Among other reasons:

- *Reduce domestic economic volatility.* Create a balanced portfolio not dependent on a single economy.
- *Increase expansion opportunities.* There are emerging, high-growth markets all over the world.
- *It's not labor intensive.* The point we're making in this chapter and book is that it's easily done with little investment, creating great potential ROI.
- *Learn continually.* You'll be exposed to diverse people, cultures, backgrounds, and opinions.

Figure 5.4: **A site offering two languages: German and English**
Reprinted with permission of Dr. Guido Quelle ©2011. All rights reserved.

· *Increase selectivity.* You have the flexibility to pick and choose your clients.
· *Stay in the game.* Your competition is already doing it or considering it.
· *Recreate.* Take your family to travel in countries where you have contacts, information, and even repute in advance.
· *Gain renown.* A global presence makes you far more attractive to local audiences and as a "sole source" to RFP (request for proposals) competitive bidding, circumventing the hoops you're asked to jump through.

The new global service provider

We've both seen a highly dramatic increase in our businesses on a global basis. Many projects have been concluded with relationships begun and sustained on Skype, blogs, websites, newsletters, forums, and product purchases.

We've been able to do this by leveraging technology. Here's what we recommend from the distillation of our successful experiences, a list of "best practices" for the new professional global services provider:

1. Use email to deliver information with brevity and speed. Try to respond within four hours during your work day.
2. Use your website to offer free resources, creating word-of-mouth and repeat visitors.
3. Utilize video conferencing tools such as www.Skype.com or www.owoo.com, among others, to conduct business meetings and/or implementations of projects. Both of us use Skype extensively to work with global prospects and clients. Skype can support ten concurrent users as we write this, and we'd guess 100 by the time some of you are reading this!
4. Instant messaging is highly effective with subcontractors, employees, and clients. Tools such as iChat can delegate and monitor projects on a real-time, frequent basis.
5. Webinars can provide interactive presentations with audio and video support. You can use tools such as www.gotomeeting.com, www.mikogo.com, or www.fuzemeeting.com, to name a few current, popular alternatives.
6. You can quickly coordinate group meetings and schedules among multiple participant calendars by using something such as www.doodle.com.
7. A site such as www.liveperson.com provides flexible tools for interaction between your customer service team and visitors.
8. Teleseminars can provide both marketing reach and income, and are now usually free to mount, using www.totallyfreeconference calls.com or www.instantteleseminar.com.
9. Live streaming of events you host locally to a global audience is now an easy reality with resources such as www.livestream.com.

To effectively obtain global business, begin by strengthening your brand locally, regionally, and domestically. Start with as strong a base as you can.

Leverage your existing clients' referrals to introduce you, proactively, to international contacts.

CASE STUDY
Who Is that Man?

Alan was running a series of executive briefings at State Street Bank when he noticed a man he had never met sitting in the rear of the room. He asked one of his contacts about this, and was told that he was the head of European operations, visiting briefly, and came to sit in the room since everyone he was supposed to meet with was in the briefing.

Alan asked for an introduction, explained during a break that everything he was talking about would apply to Europe, and then sustained an email correspondence. Two months later, he had State Street Europe included in his expanding project and revenues.

Publishing a book is enormously helpful in international work. Alan has had his books translated into ten languages so far, and had one published, with co-author Omar Khan, a Pakistani, in Singapore. It's a good idea to approach editors in other countries via the web, and always let them know if you'll "be in town."

Act like you're a global provider, don't just talk about it.

Virtual Reality

If you maintain global electronic contacts, people act as though they already know you and will be highly amenable to personal visits should you want to make them.

Here's Phil Symchych, president of Symco & Co., management consultants in Regina, Canada:

I have regular video coaching and mentoring sessions with my clients using Skype. These video calls help me interpret my client's reactions, see their environment, and make a strong personal connection. During a recent conversation, I drew up a process visual on the fun vs. profit double axis chart and held it up to the camera. My mentoree, on the other side of the world, suddenly smiles and nods as he reaches a new level of understanding. That's priceless.

The myth of cultural differences

Culture is collapsing.

Before *you* collapse in indignation, let's explain what that means for you and web communities. Entrepreneurs are entrepreneurs all over the world. Our commonalities include:

- Desire to dramatically grow our businesses
- Passion for innovation, change, and challenge
- Intent to operate on a global basis
- Want to own what we create
- Seek diverse clients and customers
- Routinely use the web to implement our strategies
- Focused on the value of improving our clients
- Seeking repeat and referral business—market gravity
- Protect quality time for our families and loved ones
- Keep stress reduced and manageable

These traits transcend borders, language (as we've pointed out above), ethnicity, background, ability, and so forth.

Our customers and clients have similar generic identities:

- Instant gratification
- Trusted providers and suppliers
- Quickly verified high credulity and relevant experiences

- Testimonials and client lists
- Evidence of thought leadership and intellectual property

People are more similar than dissimilar.

Alan has been to 59 countries. The following he'll provide in the first person.

59 countries and their commonalities

My experience is that there is an accelerating need for people all over the world to learn more. This is exacerbated by access to the web; the proliferation of younger people in developing countries; faster and easier travel; and globalized businesses.

In Iran alone, just to take one example, *two-thirds of the population is younger than 30!*

Applied to the United States, that would be over 200 million people, by comparison. People are hungry for learning, have means to access learning globally, and can readily see the divide between those with knowledge and those without. The new "discrimination" will not be by the color of one's skin or background, but rather by the education (formal and/or informal) that represents high potential for success.[1]

Cultural differences are largely overdone.

One stereotype is that the Japanese will not speak out or participate in terms of giving an opinion in front of groups. But the simple way to deal with that is by forming small groups and allowing a spokesperson to report the group's consensus recommendations without necessarily claiming it as his or her own. But I've found many groups in the U.S. to be the same way.

The web, of course, enables all of us to participate equally. (Hence, the famous cartoon of two dogs at a keyboard thinking, "On the internet, no one knows you're a dog.") I've found that there are higher penetrations of cell phone use (per capita) in several countries outside

---

[1] This is why inferior schools and teachers in poor areas are an institutional form of discrimination.

of the U.S. Authorities such as W. Edwards Deming and his quality work took off in Japan much earlier than in the United States or elsewhere. There is more ease of finding wifi connections—and for free—in many European countries.

I've used the internet without interruption from a mountaintop bungalow in St. Lucia; from a cottage on stilts over the water in Bora Bora; from an ancient monastery in France; and from airplanes flying over the Atlantic and Pacific oceans.

Knowledge and learning are becoming the great common denominator, and the internet has become the fundamental vehicle.

Virtual Reality

Focus on similarities. We all smile the same way. We all cry similar tears. And we all have predominantly the same kinds of development needs.

We've coached a wide variety of people who specialize in global work, that is, *how* to do global work, so there is apparently a great market to teach people how to do business globally.

We'd like to suggest to you how to overcome the myths of "this won't work here."

Here are five tips for dealing with some actual cultural differences. We provide these so that you're not dissuaded from "going global" by myths and urban legends.

1. If you find one or two other languages particularly attractive (because they're spoken in areas of high potential for your goods and services), then consider offering other languages on your site at least for major areas. If you look at many sites originating in Quebec, for example, you'll find options to click on French or English.

CASE STUDY
Why It Can't Work in Germany Until It Does

Alan had been asked for years how to implement value-based fees in Germany where, it was claimed, there was no precedent, no prospect of acceptance from clients, and no appreciation of the benefits. Consultant after consultant, firm after firm, said, "It makes sense, but it won't work here."

Then along came Dr. Guido Quelle, CEO of Mandat in Dortmund (whose website page appears in Figure 5.4), and he decided to simply "do it." Within a year, his entire seven-euro annual revenue was transferred to a 100-percent value-based fees approach.

If you think something can work, or if you think it can't work, you're probably right.

2. You can readily find people who will translate your major works (e.g., promotional literature, manuals, web pages, and so forth) so that you can gradually transition your work.

3. Minimize jargon, acronyms, slang, and local references. Even for those fluent in English, it can be difficult and even obnoxious to try to deal with these colloquialisms and idioms.

4. Solicit position papers and reports from others in various languages and post them on your site with a menu item such as "Position papers in other languages."

5. Consider your intended audience and put yourself in their shoes. Don't assume that they have a frame of reference identical to your local audience. Consider using their frame of reference for examples, analogies, and metaphors. (Example: Don't use baseball analogies, which are not understood in many countries.)

There are about 200 million blogs in the world as we write this. People all over the earth are blogging and commenting, overwhelmingly

---

CASE STUDY
State Street and the Common Language

While working on a global project for State Street Bank, headquartered in Boston, our first stop was London, where we expected the least cultural issues. What we found was a hornet's nest.

How could our relatively common language cause an image problem? Then the local general manger cited the latest marketing material published by the corporate brain trust. It was accurate in terms of products and services offered, but on the final page we all gasped at the contact information: It was the Boston office! There was never an alteration made for any of the far-flung operations around the globe.

---

in English. That's the benefit at the moment. What will make you stand out in a crowd? Adding cultural and linguistic understanding.

At this writing, one of Alan's books is being translated into Portuguese, which is the tenth language in which his work appears.

Invoicing and collecting internationally

You have to get paid, and it's a tad more difficult internationally. But here are some tips.

Credit cards

You'll need a secure page on your website to collect and process credit cards. You can set up payments in several ways:

- Use a service such as PayPal (www.PayPal.com) to actually process the credit cards and gain approval. Funds are then held in an internet account from which you can draw them or leave them until needed. You can also use the account to directly pay for items you purchase at sites using the same system. This is easy and automated. But the downside is a delay in receiving funds, and not everyone ordering will have a PayPal account, meaning they'd have to create one. That might turn away some purchasers.

· Use a service such as 1ShoppingCart (www.1shopping cart.com), which accepts orders, acknowledges them, and lists them for your downloading. You can then manually process the credit cards on a "hard" or virtual terminal.

· Use a system such as WorldPay (www.worldpay.us/), which allows you to process credit cards immediately on your computer.

· Set up a merchant account for Visa and MasterCard using your merchant bank. If you have accounts there, the bank will usually provide the necessary connections. A terminal will be sent to you.

· Separately, go to American Express to gain acceptance for their cards. It helps tremendously if you have American Express accounts yourself.

Payment by credit card is very efficient for international transactions, and the cost of doing business (generally 2.3 to 3.5 percent per transaction) is reasonable. (Never charge more for a credit card purchase, which is highly amateurish.) We've done business with clients such as the United States Air National Guard and Toyota, who prefer to pay with credit cards (often avoiding their own internal, bureaucratic purchasing procedures.)

If you receive very large orders from individuals you don't know—especially in parts of Africa and Russia—it's a good idea to request a faxed ID and copy of the card, since card theft is unfortunately rife in those areas, and you would have otherwise shipped the products and only learn of the non-acceptance of the charge weeks later when the bill goes to the real cardholder.

Wire transfers

Another source of collection is by wire transfer. You bank will have a "Swift" number for domestic wire transfers (it's usually the numbers to the left of your account number on the bottom of your checks), but a separate routing number for international wire transfers. You'll have to call your bank to obtain that. By providing your bank's name, account number, address, phone number, wire transfer number, and often a manager's name, the wire can be processed usually within a week, and often as quickly as 48 hours. There is a charge to do this which you'll have to absorb, based on the amount of the check. A downside here is that you have to know and trust the other party, since this information does provide access to your account number and bank.

Checks

You can accept checks, but keep these criteria in mind:

· The check must be in U.S. (or whatever your currency is) funds.
· The check must be drawn on an American (or local) bank. Most foreign banks have relationships with local ones, so that the corresponding bank can honor the U.S. funds.
· Always have the check sent by FedEx overnight service, never by regular mail.

Virtual Reality

Stop worrying about exchange rates and credit card processing fees. They are a cost of doing business, not a reason to turn away business!

Wait for a check to be processed and deposited into your account before delivering services or shipping products. This process takes about a week (and isn't necessary if you know the other party well).

It is generally not a good idea to open local bank accounts in other countries, since there are often taxes, interest, and restrictions on moving funds around, and it may make you a target in the local tax system as a foreigner who set up a business in the local country. That will never have a happy ending.

CASE STUDY
Canada Is So Close But So Far Away

A client's assistant sent a check for $25,000 as promised. It was marked "U.S. funds." Our bank accepted the deposit, but it didn't show up in the online account, and after several days I called the bank manager.

I was told that there was no corresponding bank, so the procedure was to *manually, by regular mail, return the check to the Vancouver bank, have it validated, and then make the funds translation and deposit, and the process takes two weeks!*

Oh, yes; the bank charged me a hefty fee for their trouble of depositing my money!

Keep tabs on the foreign exchange

It is helpful to watch exchange rates in terms of marketing opportunities. For example, we've run large workshops in Australia when that dollar was well below the U.S. dollar, and costs of doing business were very inexpensive. The downside is the fees charged to participants, which are perceived as quite high. Conversely, we've marketed work in Australia six months ahead of the designated visit because the Australian dollar was so strong it was on par with the U.S. dollar, enabling more people to sign up locally. The additional revenues more than offset the additional costs.

Share your global friendliness

It's important to make it evident on your site that you are globally friendly to do business with. Your ordering pages should verify they're secure by the designation "https," and not merely the traditional "http." You should have testimonials from all over the globe. Your examples should be universal and generic.

Profit-sharing offers, bartering, and cold hard cash

Never accept offers to travel somewhere and "share in the profits." Like a Hollywood film that does $45 million at the box office but never shows a bottom-line profit with which to pay the investors, you'll find that your local hosts' expenses will engulf all revenues, leaving you with your own air fare to pay and not a cent of profit.

In fact, with the exception of small product sales, *always* demand full payment before you arrive. For example, in speaking for groups in Melbourne and Sydney, we ask for a 50-percent deposit on booking, and the balance two weeks in advance of our leaving on the trip. We also request full expense payment in advance, at least for the airline tickets.[2] Don't use or trust local "brokers" to collect and hold your money.

Some people will want to barter, claiming it's "easier" than international cash transactions. (Translation: They have no cash with which to transact.) We know someone who accepted $50,000 in Philippine hand-woven baskets, since cash was not available. At last check, those baskets had collapsed in a warehouse in Arizona.

You want to collect cash. You can do so with credit card, wire transfer, or check if you take appropriate precautions.

Collecting on the internet is the best and most efficient alternative. We suggest that you accept PayPal *as well as* offer merchant credit card accounts. (You could also include "minor cards" such as Discover.) The transaction is the most customer-friendly. Make sure you indicate clearly on your buying sites that the prices are in "U.S. funds," or whatever funds you prefer. You can put a link to a currency translator right on the site, so that anyone can figure out very quickly what the fee or price is in local currency.

Do everything possible to prevent bad debts. Trying to collect them is difficult enough locally, and often virtually impossible internationally. To quote Cuba Gooding, Jr. in the movie *Jerry Maguire*, "Show me the money!"

---

[2] Currently, a first-class ticket to Sydney from New York is more than $26,000.

Blogs, Bogs, and Fogs

is there far too much "air time"?

Gutenberg's latest iteration

Prior to the creation of movable type in the mid-15th century, monks took years to copy text and artwork that only the nobility could afford to purchase (and many of them couldn't even read them). The printing press enabled the masses to seek literacy so that they could read the Bible and engage more intimately in their religion.

However, it also created the first means for the rapid (in those times, breathtaking) dissemination of knowledge, and the means for people to communicate with each other. From the time of St. Paul's vociferous letter writing, which constituted the first nascent leveraged communities ("pass on this letter to others"), nothing much had changed in terms of communication over 14 centuries. Post-Gutenberg, people could do more than learn—the could *teach* on a large scale and create uniform learning and teaching vehicles.

It's no coincidence that Matt Mullenweg's creation of the most popular blogging platform in the world is "WordPress," a term that provides continuity from the printing press. We now have the most astounding press ever at our fingertips enabling everyone to become a writer, editor, and publisher. Whereas before now, the creation and the printing and the distribution were separate events conducted by different sources, today they are inextricably entwined in a single source: you, sitting at a keyboard.

Ironically, like those ancient monks, you're sitting at a platform with a writing implement. But your words are immediately broadcast, your sentiments instantly transferred. (Of course, that can be a blessing and a bane. The monks never regretted hitting "send" too soon.)

CASE STUDY
Alan's Blog

I was opposed to blogging as the popularity grew because I saw so much of it as a "time dump." At the time there were perhaps half as many blogs as today, and almost all the ones I reviewed were awful, both from a content and a style aspect. People seemed to be sating their egos.

But Chad convinced me to at least try one about six years ago. He created a WordPress platform for us, and the rest is, well, written on the blog. I post 4 to 5 times a week, mixing text, guest columns, podcasts, video, even cartoons ("The Adventures of Koufax and Buddy Beagle," my dogs, now well over 100 weeks and growing). Chad also recommended that we accept commentary and that I respond to it.

Among my peers who lead clear niches—Marshall Goldsmith in coaching, Jeff Gitomer in sales, Seth Godin in creativity, Marcus Buckingham in individual growth, and so on—I am by far the most accessible. The blog has become a central marketing tool for my mentoring, coaching, workshops, consulting, products, and other services. And it's become a regular part of my business day.

Blogs were originally "web logs," and began as a means for individuals to create a personalized online diary which displayed each post in descending order from most recent to the original. Over the years, they've evolved in strength, robustness, and popularity (200 million and growing, globally, as we write this). Although the vast preponderance are idiosyncratic, ego-driven, and outright bloviation, a small percent are outstanding to the point of being central learning and teaching points in people's careers and lives.

To be fair, there are other good blogging platforms, such as TypePad and Blogger, and probably others created since we've written this. But here are the traits of a WordPress blog that make the most sense for you:

- *Robustness*. The platform is constantly improving with a huge community of users and developers.
- *Plugins*. These are open source programs, written by individuals worldwide, that perform certain functions and add that functionality as an integrated part of your blog. There is a plugin directory you should consult at http://wordpress.org/extend/plugins, which provides a history of updates, support, and popularity. Some of the more useful and popular include:
  - *Spam: NoSpamNX*. Uses an ingenious method of trapping spam bots (robots) that flood sites with worthless comments.
  - *Contact: Fast Secure Contact Form*. Allows the flexibility of adding custom fields to contact forms.
  - *Sociable*. Used to add social networking connections to blog posts.
  - *WP-Print*. Enables printing of threads.
  - *WP-email*. Enables emails of threads to others.
  - *Twitter: The Wickett Twitter Widget*. Enables visitors to tweet posts.
  - *SEO: All in one SEO*. A great blend of features for search engine optimization. It also gives you the option to have the plugin generate descriptions specific to pages, as well as add

keywords of your own or description of your own on individual pages that you create.

- *Software evolution.* Over the years the platform has improved dramatically so that we now use WordPress not only as the engine for blogs but also the engine that empowers our clients' robust websites:

  - *Themes.* Wide range of designs are available to make your blog look more professional.
  - *Hosting.* It offers a hosted version on www.WordPress.com which you can create very quickly or a self-hosted version which you may then create and implement on your own server. To create the utmost flexibility, reduce vulnerability, and brand your own URL, we recommend you host your blog and site on your own server or chosen Internet Service Provider (ISP).
  - *Experts.* A large amount of developers (such as Chad's organization) are available to review your business strategy and objectives and then design and customize a robust and unique blog or site to achieve greater success.

Blogs give you the ability to quickly start creating the ultimate repository of your intellectual property. What should your blog include and what are the benefits of blogging?

- It gives you the utmost flexibility in creating your content without having to contact your web person. It enables rapid publishing and reduces dependency on your web team.
- To improve the user's experience you may easily incorporate text, photos and images (one-dimensional), audio recording (two-dimensional), and videos (three-dimensional), as Alan's case study demonstrated.
- It allows you to present fresh, new ideas with formal and informal viewpoints on various topics you and your audiences are interested in. You are then able to increase your credibility and trust, start positioning yourself as an expert in your field, and build your thought leadership.

- It opens up a communication channel with your audience to enable discussions between you and your audience *and among them,* and start building a community around your brand.
- It enables visitors to follow your blog in their preferred way. For example, they can visit your blog when they choose by simply launching their browser and selecting your domain name. They may register through RSS (Really Simple Syndication), which then enables them to read your blog and others' blogs through their preferred aggregator such as Google Reader, www.google.com/reader, or they may subscribe to your blog via email subscription with integrated tools such as FeedBurner, www.feedburner.google.com.
- It provides you with the ability to listen to the pulse of your buyers and hear their discussions and recommendations for improvement.
- It enables great ways of indexing, categorizing, and searching your content.
- You may invite guest contributors to increase and improve your content and increase visibility.
- It provides rich links to additional resources, but with value accrued to you.
- It improves your search engine ranking and global exposure.
- It becomes your accountability partner, which then helps foster digital accountability to force you to create and repurpose content.
- Because your competitors are already doing so!

Who could benefit from the implementation of a blog? We believe that entrepreneurs, consultants, advisors, coaches, speakers, attorneys—anyone offering professional and personal services, especially on a non-commodity basis, but also organizations seeking better means to market to their communities, which can then become interactive.

To maximize your blog success, you have to be passionate—committed to it—and not merely complying with normative pressure (everyone has one so you need one, too). You have to be willing to write, record, and post often—at least three times a week. You must be open-minded and generous, and embrace differing opinions and values. That means you must be able to accept critique, and not see the blog as adversarial, but rather collegial.

And you have to be willing to grow as the technologies grow and improve.

We've included four screenshots below, representing successful blogs in our estimation. Take a look, then we'll note the best practices.

Figure 6.1: **Successful blog #1**
Reprinted with permission of Stuart Cross ©2011. All rights reserved.

Figure 6.2: **Successful blog #2**

The best practices you'll see common to all the web pages in Figures 6.1 to 6.4 are:

· Profession and clean—world-class look.
· Distinguished content in terms of articles, images, charts, links, podcasts, and videos.
· Announcements of events, workshops, teleseminars, books, testimonials, and so on.
· Promotion of products and services in the margins.
· Consistent and frequent posts.

Figure 6.3: **Successful blog #3**
Reprinted with permission of Phil Symchych ©2011. All rights reserved.

- Integration with social media platforms.
- Open for comments and interaction, which creates a sense of community.
- Provocative, entertaining, and helpful.

Use our bullet points to go back and review the blogs above (or go to them online), and you can see the success in action.

Figure 6.4: **Successful blog #4**
Reprinted with permission of Brad Cleveland ©2011. All rights reserved.

(Beyond the blogs: WordPress, as indicated, enables these types of features but also can launch powerful websites, as well.)

People still visit coffee shops to meet, exchange ideas, find out what's new, and interact. They still do, but it's more often their iPad or other smart device that is the source of their information and exchanges. In fact, we see a great many people having coffee in these shops while using their smart devices, making coffee and a seat (and internet access) the main draw.

Are they reading about you on that iPad, hearing you, watching you? Are you leveraging these technologies to be in the coffee shop with them virtually, in Hong Kong, Sydney, Toronto, Berlin, and New York?

Talking heads

How many times have you visited websites that attempt to use video as an enticement, only to turn you off and send you away? If you do stay, you want to somehow wreak havoc with the image on the screen!

Why are we glued to the screen at some points and repelled at others? How do we separate ourselves from others and avoid the dreaded "talking head" syndrome?

Please take a moment when you can to review these three YouTube channels:

1. www.youtube.com/user/BuyGitomer
2. www.youtube.com/user/BatesComm
3. www.youtube.com/user/alansummitconsulting

If you can do this immediately, do so, and we'll be waiting here when you return. Otherwise, you may want to put the book down and return to it once you've had a chance to watch the videos.

What are your conclusions about the quality and interest generated? Write down three commonalities you observe having watched them:

1. _____

2. _____

3. _____

To stand out in a crowd you must have something valuable, interesting, provocative, and/or remarkable to say. And you must do so with an infectious enthusiasm. The reaction can't be, "So what?" but must be "How do I get more?!"

Otherwise, you're just one of the crowd.

Equipment to help you stand out

Invest in top-flight equipment (or hire someone who does). You'll need a high definition (HD) video camera, microphone, and lighting. (This latter is not as simple as turning on a light or moving outdoors. Take a look at the lighting array at the next play or performance you attend. It's an art form.) Great gear is more economical today than ever before as demand and competition increase. Yet we still see an overwhelming assortment of amateur efforts, which are demeaning.

Here is a brief list of our recommended equipment:

1. *Audio Mixer.* Use to connect the digital recorder with the wireless microphone as well as another handheld microphone that you can pass to the audience during a workshop. We use the Behringer XENYX 802 8-Channel Compact Audio Mixer.

2. *Digital Camera.* Use this for high-end photos. This amazing camera can also take HD videos. We use the Canon EOS 7D SLR Digital Camera.

3. *Digital Recorder.* Use to record your workshops as well as phone interviews in high quality. We recommend the Marantz PDM620.

4. *iPhone.* Use it to also record client video testimonials when you don't have the other video recorder easily available.

5. *Telephone Handset Audio Interface.* Use to connect your landline to the digital record, to record your phone interview with high-end quality. We recommend Quicktap JK Audio.

6. *Video Camera.* Use to video record your workshops, high-end video testimonials, and short video promo clips for your products and services. We use the Canon VIXIA HF21 Dual Flash Memory Camcorder.

7. *Wireless Handheld Microphone.* Use this wireless microphone to pass among the audience members during your workshops. We use Azden 105HT–105 Series UHF Wireless Microphone System with 15HT Handheld Transmitter.

8. *Wireless Microphone.* Use to connect this wireless microphone with a lavalier microphone, which connects the presenter to the digital recorder, in very high sound quality. We use Sennheiser EW112-p G3 Camera Mount Wireless Microphone System with ME2 Lavalier Mic (A / 516–558 MHz).

Although not really specified as equipment, we should also mention here that we use http://totallyfreeconferencecalls.com to record our phone interviews, which allows us to save the calls and then download them as WAV files that can easily be converted to MP3 files.

You also need to look like a pro. This, too, isn't as easy as it looks. Consult an image expert to find your best colors and ask your videographer for help with on-camera results. For example, white shirts and blouses often don't show well on video, contrary to what you might believe. Haircut, makeup, and jewelry are other considerations. You even need to consider whether your shoes are going to be in the shot.

Craft your script and video

Develop an outline for your presentation. If you're using a videographer, ask if a teleprompter is available, since you can read your notes right on the camera. If not, place notes slightly off-camera or on a surface in front of you. Some people use a recorder with an ear plug to prompt them. Others simply memorize. Do what's comfortable for you.

To create your "script":

- Start with your premise and/or title.
- Develop your key points in sequence.
- Develop at least one example for each point.
- Assemble any props you need (to take advantage of the medium).
- Practice transitions from one point to the next.
- Develop your opening and closing comments.[1]
- Rehearse your blocking, movements, and gestures in front of the camera.

Typically, promotional videos and testimonials are best kept to less than a minute; informative videos are best within five minutes;

---

[1] Make sure your opening is enticing and strong. People decide in the first 90 seconds whether to listen to what follows.

Virtual Reality

Some videos are more effective as "less than professional," *ad hoc* segments, which highlight the realism. Testimonials shot at a client site or event fall into this category. You can use a personal camera or even your iPhone.

humorous and offbeat videos, within ten minutes. (At this writing, YouTube has an eight-minute maximum for single videos.)

You're better off with many short videos than one long one, allowing you to entice different interests if any one isn't applicable to a particular audience. There are four effective styles of delivery we've observed:

1. Look directly at the camera and speak as if conversing with one person. The most natural way to accomplish this is to create bullet point reminders, which force you to speak extemporaneously around each point.
2. A *60 Minutes* interview style in which someone asks you questions on camera. When you edit it, you can include the interviewer or just use the voice off-camera.
3. You interview others as guest contributors while the camera shoots both of you.
4. During live events, record the action and create short, powerful video "bytes," as well as lengthier segments.

These techniques, professional approaches, and preparation will help you stand out in any crowd. There is strong evidence that videos are extremely popular with search engines as well as individuals. YouTube is one of the top three search engines in the world, which means people are seeking high-quality content there. Google serves videos at the top of the search when results are shown.

You must increase your video presence if you are to increase your web presence in the foreseeable future.

Create your own broadcast central

For years, we've been accustomed to receiving broadcasts of news, entertainment, and learning from platforms such as radio and TV. The internet has completely revolutionized this. Think about satellite radios such as Sirius XM Radio or digital TV companies such as AT&T U-verse, Dish Network, Direct TV, Apple TV, and cable, among others. They are all there to provide us with options to listen and watch predetermined programs that we may seek or that may newly appeal to us. Premium channels have been created to provide us with commercial-free high-end content and on-demand, instant access to content we want.

With the revolution of the internet, we now have access to millions of broadcast channels pushing and pulling content our way (some remarkable and some not so). The new broadcast platforms are websites, blogs, mobile devices, apps, iPad, YouTube, iTunes, and Blog Talk Radio, which are represented here on behalf of many others. What are YOU doing to be a part of this broadcast revolution? *Have you created your own broadcast channels or stations yet?* Have you invited your audience to listen and watch your content? If not, what are you waiting for?

Let's first take a look at leveraging broadcast technologies to enjoy and improve your life and business. Technologies such as Pandora (www.pandora.com) and especially Apple TV (www.apple.com/appletv) in combination with Netflix (www.netflix.com) and iTunes (www.apple.com/itunes) have now provided us with utmost flexibility and have taken the concept of instant access to content to a new and higher level on a scale never before available.

Next is really some cool stuff so please read on and let us articulate further with some great examples: Chad has taken his huge library of movies and professional videos he has collected over the years on DVDs, and converted them to digital files such as MP4 or M4V (other formats are available) using tools such as Hand Brake (http://handbrake.fr) or DVD ripper from iSkySoft (www.iskysoft.com), and he has also taken his audio books purchased through Audible (www.audible.com), and his music and audio CDs and brought them all into iTunes to organize his digital repository. He has then placed all of his audio and video content of workshops and teleseminars conducted by him, Alan, and others, and imported and categorized them as playlists in iTunes. All are now physically stored on his main Mac computer.

By turning on the "home sharing" option in iTunes, his library of thousands of digital files becomes an amazing repository of entertainment enjoyment, learning, research, and business and life improvement. By turning on the "home sharing" option in iTunes, his library of thousands of digital files becomes an amazing repository of entertainment enjoyment, learning, research, and business and life improvement (see Figure 6.5). Chad can now access this library from his desktops, laptops, iPad, iPhone, or place many of these selections on his mobile devices and enjoy the experience while traveling. And since the Apple TV device is connected to several of his digital TVs, he can access this library from these TVs as well as access thousands of movies on Netflix or purchase or rent on iTunes for immediate access.

Figure 6.5: **Audiobook selections**

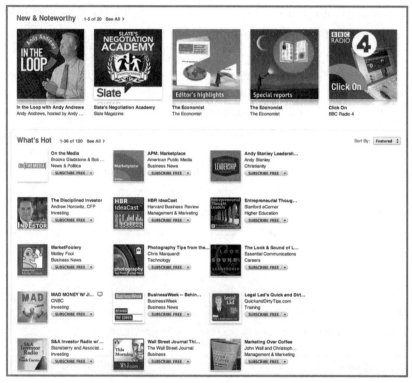

Figure 6.6: **Business podcasts examples**

Why not create your own repository for intellectual property for easy access and retrieval?

iPad and its app companions are an absolute game changer. We have written about this on our blogs (search for iPad) on www.chadbarr.com and www.contrarianconsulting.com and we recommend you look at this technology from your own usage perspective as well as broadcasting your content there. Here are some reasons why this technology is simply great:

· It is both a touch and type experience, which is innovative and enables quick access and retrieval.

· Reading newspapers such as *The Wall Street Journal, The New York Times*, and magazines such as *Business Week* and others are now fabulous digital experiences combining the power of audio and video and allowing you to obtain and read your publications anywhere and anytime worldwide.

· You gain immediate access to thousands of book titles through the iBooks app, which allows you to store and enjoy your titles digitally while "lightly" carrying them all with you.

· It takes seconds to download a desired application and start using it immediately.

· You can record both audio and video events and send them to others or upload them to your blog.

· You can watch channels such as CNN, ABC News, NPR, and even your favorite shows such as *60 Minutes* at your leisure.

Organizations and entrepreneurs have been moving aggressively to engage their audiences on this platform. Are you planning on developing your own apps to increase your broadcast reach and benefit your clients? We are, and so should you.

iTunes and podcasts

We've talked about the power of iTunes as the repository of your intellectual property and entertainment media. iTunes has become one of the largest global repositories of diverse, eclectic, and monumental intellectual property. Apple has done a remarkable job not only allowing us to purchase digital media but also assembling uniquely configured free digital content. iTunes has become of the largest repositories of diverse, eclectic, and monumental intellectual property (see Figure 6.6).

Since this book is about increasing your success and reach, if you already have established your presence on iTunes and are adding to it consistently, you are then one of the few leading the way. Otherwise, we encourage you to take action now. Once your audio podcast has been recorded, upload it to your blog or your WordPress website. Also make sure that your webmaster has created the interface from your blog to iTunes. We recommend you implement either the "podcasting" or "podpress" plugin for your WordPress blog or site. Once that integration is made, the beauty is that as soon as you upload your podcast to your blog or site, *it will be automatically distributed and posted in the iTunes podcasts repository, therefore making your content available on your site and iTunes.* Please review and learn from our own podcasts on iTunes by searching for "Chad Barr" or "Alan Weiss."

In order to broadcast yourself, you need to learn how to record your podcasts, which is quite easy today. Here are our recommendations:

·   Some of our favorite software solutions that we recommend for recording are: GarageBand, Roxio, and Audacity.
·   You should also invest in a good microphone, and we recommend you check out the USB microphones from Rode Podcaster or Snowball, as well as a stand or a small tripod kit to support it.
·   Although programs like GarageBand already come preloaded with background music and sound effects to incorporate into your recording, also look at The Music Bakery site (www.musicbakery.com), which is one of our favorite places to purchase terrific music to add to your podcasts.
·   In order to record workshops, we have used a digital recorder such as the Marantz PMD620, which does a great job in high quality and with the proper memory card stores hundreds of hours.
·   We also recommend the Sennheiser camera-mount wireless microphone system with lavaliere mike, which is a very high-quality microphone system.

Blog Talk Radio

Blog Talk Radio is a technology that allows you to easily and quickly record your podcasts using your phone directly with your online channel with no other equipment necessary. You may then embed the recording on your site or refer to this outside channel from your site. See Figure 6.7, which demonstrates the use of Blog Talk Radio with our client, Kelli Richards.

Figure 6.7: **Kelli Richards on Blog Talk Radio**
Reprinted with permission of Kelli Richards ©2011. All rights reserved.

Just as we have described the power of iTunes as a publishing platform for your content, YouTube is a powerful broadcast platform that you must participate in. Set up your dedicated channel and start uploading varied videos of your content and clients' testimonials. Figure 6.8 on page 120 shows what we've done with Alan's YouTube channel. Over five years ago, we started shooting the Writing on the Wall monthly video series. Alan shoots five at a time and we load them all to YouTube, yet release only one per moth. Each month we release the video embedded on the blog as well as on Alan's main site. We then announce it on social media as well as in Alan's *Balancing Act* monthly newsletter. We have also secured a URL, www.AlanWeiss.TV, that redirects website visitors to this channel.

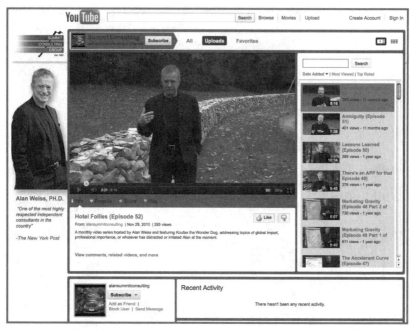

Figure 6.8: **Alan's YouTube channel**

Audible

Many like to listen to books rather than read them, and www.Audible.com is an example of such a service. Not only should you check this out if you enjoy listening to books, *but you should consider having your books available there as well and let them broadcast your message for others to discover and purchase.*

Flickr and other photo-sharing sites

You may share your photography images on platforms such as www. flickr.com among quite a few others. Our recommendation is to leverage such platforms to broadcast your events' photos of you in action, with your clients, and other interesting individuals. You may embed these images on your site.

Live Stream

Live Stream (www.livestream.com) is a service that enables you to broadcast your events live to the world. It is just like having your own TV

Virtual Reality

You are your own actor, writer, director, and producer. You might as well get good at it.

channel for truly a fraction of the cost. All you need is your video camera, a computer, a fast internet connection, their service, and *voilà*, you, too, can broadcast like the pros. Think about it: Say you conduct a live workshop that attracts 50 attendees. What if you were to offer to others the ability to watch the workshop in real time using their internet connection *and even participate* by either typing their question or calling a special phone line? This is what we call web leverage. Yet the final beauty of this solution is that you may record your workshop and make it available for future online view through this service, which is then triple leverage.

We have recently launched our new offerings, which we believe are the future of learning and interaction for entrepreneurs worldwide. Alan & The Gang (www.alanandthegang.com) is our recent invention, which contains (as of this writing) over 700 pages of video and audio pages from workshops and special high-end events conducted primarily by Alan and some of the gang members who are some of the most successful consultants and entrepreneurs in our global community. This will enable entrepreneurs to subscribe to the site, then view and search remarkable content on various topics such as: marketing, entrepreneurship, best practices, consulting, leadership, life balance, self-development, speaking, and more. It also enables them to submit questions to Alan or the gang members (see Figure 6.9, page 122).

The old days of watching "Uncle Miltie" (Milton Berle) at a fixed time, on a tiny screen in black and white, broadcast from a studio with immense cameras and tons of equipment, has given way in many of our lifetimes to someone sitting in a small room broadcasting in multimedia globally at that person's whim.

Welcome to what we call "broadcast central." Now, how do you look good when you're "on"?

Figure 6.9: **Alan & the Gang, a global learning site with multi-media**

Automated calling cards

During a recent random audit, the state's auditor asked for business cards from our major clients. Shocked, we asked what decade she wanted them from.

Remember the days when you opened up your mailbox only to find a huge amount of junk mail from companies and individuals you have never heard of before, or ones you have and would never do business with? Remember also finding the large merchandise catalogs taking most of the physical space of your mailbox, which now typically end up in the garbage?

How about your phone ringing with automated messages about vacations, better mortgages, and even a political candidate begging for your vote, and the radio and TV stations increasing their funding by attracting sponsors that bombarded us with obnoxious commercials?

The internet revolution has continued the trend of enabling companies and individuals to adapt such "interruption-based" methodologies by broadcasting spam email, unwanted newsletters, banners, and advertising on websites, as well as commercials on videos and even selling your private online information to others. Although all these are forms of automation with an attempt to reach and touch consumers, people have become savvier and have implemented ways to block these messages. Consumers have now taken control into their hands and can now decide and customize if and how they want to listen to us, how often they want to listen, as well as choose the method to do so.

Virtual Reality

You not only have to reach your audience, you have to do so in a manner that impels them to want to listen.

Think about it; we all register to receive bank alerts, stock recommendations, topics from trusted and credible sources. Businesses even leverage such alerts automation to advise their teams of financial situations, reporting, and trends. Let's explore now some options of items that can go out regularly, ideas for automating the process of reaching your audience and how to do so effectively.

Although the focus of our next chapter is on newsletters as a means of "pushing" content to your audience, let's discuss some basic principles here. The key, of course, is to never spam,[2] provide consistent value, and enable the recipient to easily accept your newsletter by opting-in or even double opting-in, or stop receiving the newsletter by opting-out. Newsletters have become increasingly popular because people still like to receive them and the ideas they provide. Whether the frequency you elect to send them is weekly, monthly, or quarterly, they automate the reach-out process from you (one) to your audience (many).

Another effective form of automation is the integration of your blog or WordPress (WP) website with iTunes. The plugin we recommend you look into integrating is "Podcasting" or "Podpress," which makes this interface easy. The beauty of this is that once the integration has been created, as soon as a podcast has been loaded on your blog or WP site, it becomes available on iTunes inside your specified channel. Here is what we recommend you do:

- Create a new brand to categorize your audio recordings.
- Create a new category on your blog to hold these recordings and name it accordingly.
- Implement the podcasting or podpress plugin on your blog or WP site.
- Register this category (feed) to iTunes, which is the Apple registry, and wait for them to approve it, which only takes a few days. This is when you also specify the description of the podcasts series as well as the accompanying image to display. For more help on this, review the Apple page: www.apple.com/itunes/podcasts/specs.html, which should clarify this interface.

---

[2] Spam, for our casual conversation here, is material sent *en masse* against arbitrary lists, without the permission of the recipient. Illegal spam has no provision to "unsubscribe" or otherwise be removed from the lists.

- Start recording your podcasts and create the files in an MP3 format.
- Post each recording on your blog or WP site, and place in the proper category.

Voilà! You are now published on iTunes and have automated the process each time a podcast is created on your blog. Visitors to iTunes can now search and find your content and, even better, register to receive automatic updates when available.

The steps above illustrate how to populate your audio content and automatically have it available on platforms such as iTunes. The same consideration should be given to serving your videos on iTunes as video podcasts.

One of the best platforms available today to showcase your videos is YouTube. As we have indicated earlier, creating your own YouTube channel will allow you to strengthen your brand, allow people to search and find your content there and automate the ability for people to register and receive announcements when you add new videos to your channel. And the best part is that embedding these videos to your sites and others sites is a snap *and you leverage Google's vast internet bandwidth rather than yours.*

Once you start creating your video content, you need to start thinking of exploiting and automating the dissemination of this content beyond your sites and YouTube. This will enable you to publish beyond your platforms and increase the possibility of people finding your content elsewhere. Quite a few options are available to automate this process, and here are the two we recommend you look into: The first one is TubeMogul (www.tubemogul.com), where you can upload your YouTube video and have it then automatically uploaded and leveraged on many other video platforms. The second is Traffic Geyser (www.trafficgeyser.com). Both of these services provide much more than just this function.

If you think of a newsletter as "push" technology, where you determine when your recipient should hopefully receive it, we would like you to think of blogs and WP sites as "pull" technology, where the recipient determines when and how to receive your content. Let's start with the non-automated method, which is mentioning your content via all possible venues. This method encourages you to reference your content by referencing links (URLs) during your video interviews, podcasts, social media output, discussions, speeches, articles, newsletters, and related vehicles. Other effective ways are the ones you integrate to your site that allow your audience to choose, such as:

- RSS feeds to receive your content through content aggregators such as Google Reader and Google Alerts.
- FeedBurner, which enables the visitor to register and receive email notifications when you post content on your blog and WP site.
- Social sharing and book marking sites integration (Digg, Stunbleupon, Delicious) so visitors may click and announce your posts to their friends.
- Tweet This, which is similar to the ones above and enables the visitor to tweet the link to your post and share with their followers.
- The Facebook "Like" button has not only gained major popularity on sites but it has now become a major influence on recommendations and purchasing power for buyers. Not only do visitors get a chance to now cast their vote by clicking on this button and sharing the content with their friends, it now shows individuals which friends of yours like the page you are on, which may be your article, products, and services. This is huge! Imagine your visitors arriving to your new announced workshop where they can see social media comments of others recommending this and also see their own friends who are attending or "liking" this page, which is a huge influencing factor.

When it comes to automatically repurposing your content, another one of our favorite methods is to automatically integrate the content of your blog and WP sites and syndicate them with the social media platforms of Twitter, Facebook, and LinkedIn. This means that as soon as you post on your blog, it will automatically post the title on Twitter and the entire post on Facebook and LinkedIn. Also, as soon as you tweet, it will post on your Facebook and LinkedIn account, and if you implement the applicable plugin on your blog, the tweets will show up there as well. To do that, you have quite a few options, yet here are the top two:

- Log on to Facebook and LinkedIn and implement their built-in apps that pull your content from your blog and Twitter. Also, implement the plugin on your blog that posts your blog titles to Twitter.
- Implement third-party solutions such as www.twitterfeed.com, which will do the entire job for you. The challenge with such solutions is that if they stop existing (always an internet hazard), you will have to replace them with another such solution or use the option specified above this one.

In the past several years we have seen a growth in automated tools that promise to populate your blog with others' content without the need for you to be involved. We advise you to stay away from such tools. The integrity of such tools is highly questionable, and the last thing you want is to be associated with content that is of low integrity.

Quite a few services exist to help you leverage your articles so they get published elsewhere. From press release services with ExpertClick.com, to many others as published by us here: www.contrarianconsulting. com/press-release-distribution-sources, to www.prleads.com as well as ezine options such as http://ezinearticles.com, and many others.

We have talked earlier about the importance of repurposing your content. Think about it: When a visitor arrives at your blog or site, the goal is to keep them there longer than not, to encourage them to return, and to have them urge others to visit. Yet since most have busy schedules, the likelihood of them reading your older content is not as great. Here are a couple of ideas to bring back the good old content and repurpose it:

- Create a category called "Best of the blog," which enables the visitors to see the best you have written. At first, simply categorize the best of your writing into this category. Later, you may also add automation tools to do this.
- Pick out an older post, perhaps even modify it by adding several more points to it, then blog about it today and the fact that you have improved the concept and then link to the old post.

The more you automate and leverage your content, the more you are able to reach your audience beyond your existing, limited capacity. So, is there "too much" air time? If provocative, fresh, helpful, and unique content is used, leveraging the concepts we've illustrated in this chapter, then we don't think there is such thing as too much air time.

On the contrary, the more valued content you use, the better and stronger you position yourself. Look at a company like Blockbuster, unfortunately not adjusting quickly enough to their customers' needs and not properly evolving with technologies, literally disappearing as we write this. But at Netflix, management has recognized the need of their customers and evolved, adjusting their technology and content distribution methods.

Are you improving and adjusting yours? If large firms can ignore the strengths and weaknesses we've covered here, certainly you can. But you can also take advantage of them to dramatically grow your business and your business communities every single day.

Newsletters: There Are Far Too Many

but only because people are reading them!

Attracting topics

What will attract people to a newsletter? Content.

"There are so many newsletters out there, why should I create one?" This is a common question we often hear from our clients. Our answer is quite simple: The reason there are so many is because people read them!

Another comment we often hear is: "I don't know what to say in my newsletters, or how to say it." Great newsletters are usually short, showcase yours and others' expertise, provide value, are provocative, look great, and encourage interaction and action. Less is usually more, which also means that your newsletter is not a vehicle to teach everything you know, but only what your readers need to know.

Keep in mind that you are not writing *War and Peace*, and getting an effective newsletter off the ground is simpler than you may think.

This chapter will provide the answers, tools, resources, examples, and best practices on how to create and greatly improve your newsletter strategy.

Virtual Reality

The more a newsletter provokes and stimulates, the more it will be of interest. Readers don't have to agree with the writer. They simply must find value in the writer's opinions and information.

What is the purpose and essence of your newsletter? It should be:

- Free, and advertised to a wide audience. We suggest you create as wide as possible appeal, and try to broaden your audience.
- Nonpromotional, except subtly and softly in terms of your valued content.
- Highly pragmatic, with insights others don't readily have.
- Brief, with four short subjects rather than one long article, thereby having an appeal to more people.
- Comprised of your intellectual property, opinion, a case study, and frequently asked questions (FAQ), for example.
- Memorable, which means at least monthly.
- Able to strengthen relationships and trust through accuracy, quality, and consistency.
- Original in building and cementing thought leadership.

Why should you consider publishing your newsletter and making the requisite time investment?

It gives you the ability to frequently and consistently "touch" your target audience, and while providing value, reminding them that you are there. Otherwise you are most likely forgotten while your competition is mostly recognized.

It enables you to showcase your expertise, points of interest, products, and services through casual mention and in the real estate in

> *"In the 4.5 years I've been in business I've gotten two 70K contracts*
> *I directly attribute to my newsletter."*
>
> —RICHARD MARTIN, PRESIDENT, ALCERA CONSULTING INC.,
> CANADA, WWW.ALCERA.CA

the margins. It gives you the ability to test new ideas and get feedback from your audience. People are very forgiving and highly supportive of free resources, which is why we advise that you never charge for a subscription. In fact, your free subscription will generate some powerful mailing lists and demographics.

The discipline forces you to create new content, preventing you from becoming stagnant. It then becomes your digital accountability partner and helps you showcase your personal style or your "voice" in your writing.

How frequently should you publish? It depends on your style and commitment. Quarterly is too infrequent and daily borders on spam (and is impossible to maintain without a staff). We recommend you start with a monthly newsletter, and once you get the hang of it and are comfortable publishing, perhaps add a special edition on "breaking developments," as well.[1]

When you consider launching your second newsletter, make sure the content and focus are uniquely different from your first newsletter, or the target audience is distinctly different. You don't want to "cannibalize" one publication for the sake of the other.

Some people are inconsistent in their publishing schedule, usually due to poor planning. Others feel it is advantageous for them to send their newsletters inconsistently at different frequencies to create a "surprise" effect. We, however, believe the key is to build consistency and clients' dependency, thus expecting your newsletter at the same

---

[1] In Alan's monthly *Balancing Act: Blending Work, Life, and Relationships,*® which has over 150 continual monthly editions at this writing, he also published special editions following 9/11 and on other occasions.

time each month. We suggest you create a regular date on which to send them out, date each issue, and put a volume and number on it (e.g., the first issue is volume 1, no. 1; the second volume 1, no. 2; the first one of the next year is volume 2, no.1, and so on).

Many of our clients debate what is the best day and time for sending their newsletter. This question rivals, in its absurdity, "When is the best day and time to play the slot machines in Vegas." Although we are sure we will be getting complaint letters from companies running statistical analyses to measure these findings, we suggest that you forget about worrying over this. Over the years and with so many of our clients, we have sent out thousands of newsletters. It is virtually meaningless to count the open rate in order to track success of your newsletter, especially since different people consume these in different manners and preferences. You should focus on delivering value, building conversations and relationships, doing so consistently and tracking the impact of your clients and revenues growth.

A great many people claim statistics showing that it's not effective to market over the summer season. Consequently, many people use this questionable claim not to market over the summer, thereby losing opportunity, momentum, and business. Publish on whatever day and whatever week you wish, just do it well!

Although we highly recommend that YOU do most of the writing for your newsletter, so you don't get overwhelmed, let's first reduce your labor intensity and discuss who may write for and contribute to your newsletter:

- The people who work with you or for you.
- Different executives inside and outside your organization (clients, prospects, colleagues, and so forth). If inside your organization, put them on a rotation for contributing. If outside, reach out to global executives and interview them on topics that may be of help and interest for your readers.
- Colleagues with whom you may have reciprocal agreements to provide articles or expertise.
- Partners. Can your spouse or significant other contribute?

- Thought leaders in your industry, especially when and if your newsletter offers them an attractive outlet for their own work.
- Clients. Co-authoring with clients is always a good idea, highly promotional in the proper manner.
- Guest contributors and interviewees. Who would make sense to feature on behalf of your thinking and your work?
- Competition. That's right, why not embrace your competition and let them contribute to your newsletters? If you think about it, notice how we ourselves have embraced our competition who have actually become our clients. This shows maturity and leadership in your field (and a lack of fear).

So now that you have solicited and have received the help of parts of this considerable universe of sources to contribute, you may be asking, "What should I write about and in what format?" We have already discussed the concepts of where ideas come from and how to provoke in order to create interest and position yourself differently and effectively. Here are some suggestions of what you should publish in your newsletters:

- What questions are your clients asking you? If you are unsure, ask them. Once you get the questions, publish the answers in your newsletters in the form of articles, tips, interviews and such.
- What topics are "hot" in your area of expertise that are being discussed in the news and media (TV, internet, radio, newspapers, and magazines) that you should also publish?
- "Live examples" from today's news sources are always a great way to illustrate and substantiate your points.
- What are the questions being asked on others' blogs or the social media platforms that would welcome your feedback (or require your contribution to the debate)?
- Showcase your expertise with ongoing ideas, innovation, opinion, and intellectual property in the form of small case studies.
- Discuss the what, how, and why as well as "dos and don'ts." The objective is to turn on the light bulb and create the "aha!" moment for the reader.

- Ask your audience questions and conduct surveys or polls and then publish results for all to benefit from.
- Shamelessly and gently promote yourself, your products, services and events. Use the end of the newsletter and/or the margins for these purposes.
- Share clients' case studies and success stories, and feature them when possible (you'll usually need permission).
- Feature interesting things on your blog and other sites of yours. Repurpose material.
- Discuss researched topics, share where you find new resources such as sites and blogs, and incorporate interesting links.

The format we recommend you use is text, interesting imagery, and process visuals as well as audios and videos. When it comes to incorporating audios and videos in your newsletter, we highly recommend you use an attractive image with an embedded link that takes you to the landing page where your media plays. This method reduces the demand that media files place on the newsletter recipient's computing resources, without affecting your excellent content.

Finally, put yourself in your intended reader's shoes. Ask yourself, "What would REALLY induce me to read something?" If you can't answer, then ask your intended audience.

Do not try to become all things to all people. Your readers will appreciate you if you keep it short as a quick read. Incorporate calls to action throughout your newsletters.

Examples of questions to provoke your audience are:

- Now that the first quarter is behind us, what are you doing to increase your success for the remainder of the year?
- Are you still waiting for the phone to ring?
- Have you reached your goals this year? If so, why not, and are you doing something about it?
- Are you surviving or thriving?

- Have you created your own best practices?
- Are you seen as a peer or a vendor?

Your subject line, other than the strength of your brand, will get your email opened and read, and is critical to create the initial interest to read your newsletter. We believe that many actually miss an opportunity to engage the reader because their subject lines are meaningless, too simplistic, or not provocative enough. So keep them short and provocative with the following examples:

- If you don't take your site seriously, why should others?
- The top five strategic internet mistakes entrepreneurs make
- Seven ways to thrive in this economy
- Is anyone listening? Why develop a brand?
- If you can drive, you can consult.
- How to say "No" and fire clients.
- How to monetize your website.
- Why do some businesses reject their clients?
- Best practices from my best clients
- If looks could kill, your clients would be dead on arrival.

> *"People may or may not read the article, but at least there's something hitting their inbox on a regular basis from me. I have been sending out my newsletter for over three years, and several times each year I get a call on the day it's delivered when someone says, "Stuart, we've got this issue and I've been thinking . . . ."*
>
> —STUART CROSS, PRESIDENT, MORGAN CROSS CONSULTING, UNITED KINGDOM, WWW.MORGANCROSS.CO.UK

Newsletters, whether hard copy or electronic, should have an ISSN (International Standard Serial Number). This is an international code that can identify any periodical, including country of source, language, and so forth. They are vital for tracking what you're doing and allowing others to find you, as well as supporting the legitimacy of your work in terms of professionalism and consistency.

The ISSN homepage is www.loc.gov/issn. This is a function of the U.S. Library of Congress, and 60 other agencies in other countries. You must submit a sample of your newsletter. The process is free, and the number assigned may be used in bar codes and other sources once issued.

Compelling formats

A while back we went to one of our favorite restaurants and noticed a new item on the menu, the Mediterranean sea bass, which was highly recommended by our waiter. We of course ordered it and concurred that it was an outstanding dish. When chatting with the waiter and commenting on his superb recommendation, he said: "You know, when we had it on the menu as 'the Bronzini' we could not sell any. So we've changed the name to 'the Mediterranean sea bass,' and we can't keep enough in stock."

So what's in a name, you ask? Everything! Your newsletter name should portray its strong focus and be memorable. Here are some examples:

- *The Voice of Business*
- *Balancing Act*
- *Great Results*
- *Sales Caffeine*
- *Take it from Terry*
- *Courageous Leadership*

Your assignment after reading the rest of this chapter is to lay out your successful newsletter design, content, and strategy if you don't have one, or to assess the effectiveness of your current strategy if you do have one. Let's also include some initial critical items to consider:

- As we have previously indicated, the subject line must grab attention and should be prominently displayed in the email and the body of the newsletter.

- The design colors should be consistent with your brand and company's look and feel.
- We prefer to keep the design width to no more than 650 pixels so it properly fits (is rendered) in most email programs. We usually use font sizes of up to 15 points for headings and up to 13 points for content.
- Use sans-serif type for headlines: Helvetica Is An Example; and serif fonts such as the one you're reading for text.
- We highly recommend you use a service to send out your newsletter, and we will discuss various options and recommendations below. Unless you have few subscribers (less than 50) and you are not planning on growing your subscriber base, do not send your newsletters directly from your email program. You may run a huge risk of being flagged as a spammer and your server may be blacklisted, which means your emails may be rejected by many recipients until you are able to white list your server again.
- Make sure your newsletter identifies you as the sender so the recipient knows from whom it is coming.
- Include a print-friendly option that allows the visitor to physically print the newsletter. (Many people like to take them along.)
- Include a table of contents at the top that when clicked on would easily position the reader at the proper section.
- Include products, videos, white papers, and events promotion in the sidebar through attractive, applicable, and clickable images.
- Incorporate social media links in your newsletter.
- Compatibility consideration must be given and ample testing of which email program may open the newsletter, as well as how it will behave on mobile devices.
- You should incorporate a link or image that says: "Having problems viewing this?" that will enable the reader to click on this link and be taken to a web page that is more likely to be read perfectly as intended.

- And finally, you should personalize your opening sentence with "Dear" followed by the person's name.

There has been an ongoing debate for years as to which newsletter format to use. Should you use a text, HTML, PDF, or even a print format for your newsletter? And the answer is: "It depends." We favor an HTML format, which has more visual diversity and aesthetically looks great. Today's newsletter can actually be formatted to look as professional and outstanding as you'd like it to be without any design limitation.

The most outstanding benefits of HTML newsletters are the fact that they look attractive and professional and they enable the inclusion of photos, images, process visuals, videos, and especially images that are clickable and not just links. The drawbacks are that HTML newsletters are more prone to be caught by anti-spam solutions, especially the ones that block images in emails, and these newsletters may be larger in size when sent via email.

Text newsletters, although not visually attractive, can be quite effective at delivering high-end value or promotion announcements without fluff. Several of our clients have chosen to also deliver their newsletter as a hard-copy print version that often looks like a glossy magazine. We have seen various degrees of success with this method and include it here for you to consider. Yet, if your audience is going "green," we suggest you stay with digital distribution only, perhaps even promote the fact that this is another way for you to go green.

As far as a PDF is concerned, we recommend using it for your newsletter archive version, which we'll cover in the next section. Finally, and when given the choice, why not provide your subscribers with options to select the one they want?

When a newsletter is sent out via email, its "digital life expectancy" is quite limited to days or weeks at best. To extend this life and effectiveness, we recommend you archive each one of your newsletters for all to easily access on your website. The benefits are several: First, it enables future visitors to read your older newsletters. Second, it increases your body of work on the web. Third, it improves your Google and other search engines ranking and therefore the search results. Fourth, it creates a repository of your intellectual property to easily access and search. Fifth, it enables you to leverage it in your discussions with clients.

You may want to consider providing an option in your archive newsletter page on the web to allow the visitor to also click on a PDF version of the newsletter. Although this creates more work, it does provide more valuable options. See how we formatted Alan's *Balancing Act* newsletter archive page in Figure 7.1.

Figure 7.1: **Archived newsletter**

An effective top banner should incorporate the following:

- Simple yet attractive design where the height of the banner is narrow, to easily fit in the email display screen and show much of the content below it.
- Display the name, essence, and focus of the newsletter or the value proposition. Tagline is optional.
- Incorporate your company's logo and the date or month and year. See the example in Figure 7.2, featuring our U.K. client, Stuart Cross, of Morgan Cross Consulting.

As your newsletter gains strength and popularity, there is a good chance that one of your subscribers may forward it to someone else. Or perhaps one decides to print it and present it in their next corporate meeting. We therefore highly suggest you include the following:

- Identifying information and an easy way to contact you via email, phone, web address.
- A way to forward the newsletter to a colleague or a friend.
- Copyright message (e.g., ©Alan Weiss 2011 or Copyright Chad Barr 2011.)
- Encourage others to distribute, copy, and print, with proper permission and attribution to you. Why not suggest the following at the bottom of your newsletter: "You are welcome to print, email, or distribute this newsletter to others. To do so, you must include our identifying information, our copyright message, as well as attribution to us." This will encourage them to pass on your message, give them the permission necessary, and create the viral effect, which is a great thing.

So how many sections should you consider including? The answer is very straightforward: "6.723!" We are just kidding of course. It actually depends primarily on your writing style, capability, and commitment. We have clients that have one section only, and some that have quite a few. Obviously, the more sections you have, the more you have to write and contribute. Choose the number that you feel will allow you to

Figure 7.2: **Newsletter banner design**
Reprinted with permission of Stuart Cross ©2011. All rights reserved.

communicate your message consistently without placing an unrealistic burden on you. Figure 7.3 shows a sample newsletter from one of our U.S. clients, Richard Citrin, of Citrin Consulting. It demonstrates some of the following best practices:

· Clear and clean design, value proposition, and corporate identity while showcasing his expertise and personal brand.

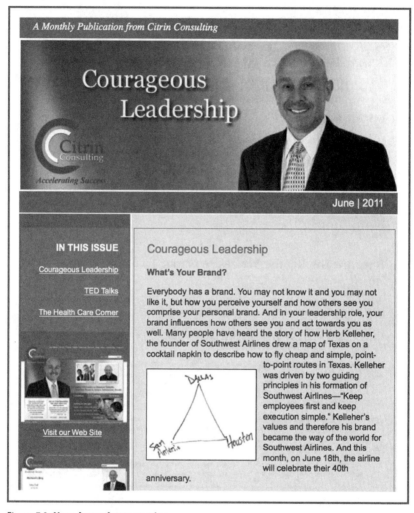

Figure 7.3: **Newsletter best practices**
Reprinted with permission of Richard Citrin ©2011. All rights reserved.

- Three sections and easy-to-access table of contents at the top.
- Margin links, both in image and text link format, to his corporate website and blog.
- Great intellectual property and inclusion of process visuals.

CASE STUDY
The Newsletter

"Write your newsletter! And do it faithfully every month." My web guru, Chad Barr, instructed me to get this task done as a first assignment to my completed website, www.citrinconsulting.com.

As I was going off to a writing workshop with Alan Weiss a couple of weeks later, I thought that would be a great opportunity to work on my newsletter draft. One of our assignments was to go outside the meeting room, spend 45 minutes, and write 600 words that you can use for a newsletter or article.

I drafted the article based on a recent experience and applied it to a business situation that was particularly cogent for a current client I was working with at the time. I kept the article brief, was able to tie business aspects into the story, and included three or four bullet points that captured key ideas that the reader could use in their professional work.

Upon returning to the group and reading my story, I got great reviews.

After a few editorial reviews I sent it on to Chad's team, who readied it for posting as my first newsletter. It went out the next week and I almost immediately received great feedback from my readers:

- "VERY COOL! Wonderful. Keep them coming."
- "I will be able to use this with an employee."
- "Terrific message, thanks for including me."

I had a great open rate, and that has continued with my newsletter. Entitled "Courageous Leadership," I address challenging issues for leaders that, I hope, provoke their thinking and support their development as leaders.

Later on, Chad reminded me, "Keep the quality and timing consistent, and use it to build intellectual property for your website." The result, he told me, would help me to build a brand that would yield results each and every month.

And that has been the case. Each month that my newsletter goes out, I get a new and unique comment from a reader. New people sign up after their

CASE STUDY, continued

colleagues pass my newsletter on to them and then they pass it on to others. Slowly but surely my network and contacts are expanding.

Today, I noticed that I had a new sign-up from a person with whom I am negotiating a new contract. She told me that she checked out my site, liked what she saw, and enjoyed reading my newsletter. She told me that she and her company were excited to be working with me and were looking forward to great things from our work together.

Whether it is a newsletter or a blog, be faithful to your work and get it done. You will see results.

—Richard Citrin, Ph.D., MBA, Citrin Consulting,
www.citrinconsulting.com

When considering the design of your newsletter, and depending on the service you elect to send out your newsletter, you are usually given the choice of selecting a template or design your own. An existing template may be just want you need to get this up and running quickly, although we must admit that most of our clients elected to have us design their own unique, branded newsletter layouts.

The other consideration is whether to include the entire newsletter content in the body of your newsletter, or display only the opening paragraph of each section, with a link to read the rest of it. There are pros and cons to each; actually, Alan's newsletter uses the former logic while Chad's newsletter uses the latter logic. The benefits of Alan's style are that the user is not forced to click on links to read the rest of each section and the entire newsletter is there for them to scroll through. The benefits of Chad's style are that the email received is usually more condensed, and that allows the reader to quickly glance at top headlines and beginning paragraphs. It then drives more traffic to the website when the reader clicks on the link to read the rest of the article. It also provides more analytical capabilities, for those interested, to track not only open rates but also which articles are being read and by whom.

You choose the method most attractive to you. See the example of Alan's successful newsletter in Figure 7.4, where we have actually

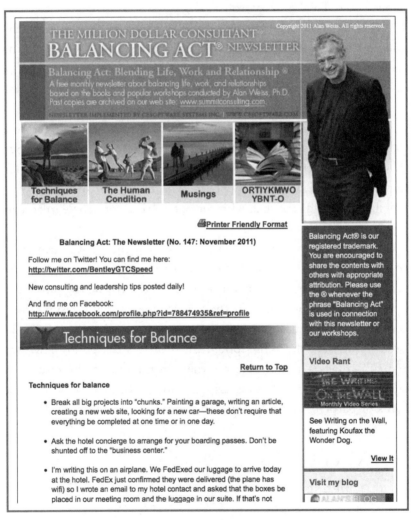

Figure 7.4: **Breaking some rules**

decided to break the rules. Notice the announcements of products and events in the margins.

Balancing Act is long, comprising three major articles or columns monthly. It also is assertively promotional, using marginal real estate to showcase new offerings. It is sent out each month as a press release on one of our services (ExpertClick.com) in its entirety. A strong brand allows you to bend or break some rules!

The sample newsletters we've demonstrated so far showcase the concepts discussed and happen to all be monthly. Although the frequency does not necessarily impact the look and feel, we do want to also show you an example of the weekly newsletter we have created for Alan, which is called *Alan's Monday Morning Memo* (see Figure 7.5).

There is a plethora of laws, some observed and some not, to protect people from spam. We encourage you to be ethical and legal about your methods of attracting and subscribing visitors to your newsletters. Your approach should be that only people who truly want to receive your newsletter should receive it, with the option then for people to accept, or opt-in, or reject, or opt-out.

Although we both completely agree that you must have permission to add a person to your distribution list, we vary a bit in our approaches. Alan places the responsibility for registration directly on the subscriber and prefers a double opt-in method, which means that the subscriber, once registered, must reply to the automatic email sent to them in order to activate the subscription. Chad prefers the philosophy that the subscriber is responsible for the registration, yet he also adds subscribers himself or has his assistant do so when receiving business cards of participants to his speaking engagements and such. He also

Virtual Reality

You're better off with a newsletter reaching 500 high-potential buyers than one reaching 10,000 irrelevant people.

Alan's Monday Morning Memo – 10/24/11

Posted on October 24, 2011 by Alan Weiss

October 24, 2011—Issue #109

This week's focus point: Business growth superstar David Maister was my guest at my annual Thought Leadership Workshop in Palm Beach last week. Among his gems: "How much you really want something will determine how hard you work to achieve it. Most of us know what to do, we just don't do it." That's why passion is so important in our personal and working lives. Don't try to make money and become passionate about it. Find your passions, engage and help others, and you'll earn a wonderful living.

Monday Morning Perspective: Whatever is morally necessary must be made politically possible. — Eugene McCarthy, when running for President.

Hear me weekly or monthly in 2012:
Friday Wrap: http://www.summitconsulting.com/seminars/friday-wrap.php
Advanced Teleconferences: http://www.summitconsulting.com/teleconference/2012.php

You may subscribe and encourage others to subscribe by clicking HERE.

Privacy statement: Our subscriber lists are never rented, sold, or loaned to any other parties for any reason.

Contact information: info@summitconsulting.com
http://www.contrarianconsulting.com
ISSN 2151-0091

© Alan Weiss 2011. All rights reserved

Figure 7.5: **A weekly newsletter**

prefers the single opt-in method to eliminate the possibility that the subscriber may not have gotten the confirmation email.

To inform the subscriber, this is the email Chad sends out:

In hopes that this may be of value to you and meets with your approval, I've added your email address to our newsletter list. This way I may stay in touch by providing you with monthly insights, tips, and strategies on various web, internet, technology, and business issues. Our newsletter, jammed with resources, focuses on providing information and value to our clients. If you do not wish to receive it, just let me know by replying to this email with the subject REMOVE or click on the unsubscribe option when you receive the newsletter.

When it comes to discussing the services to send out your newsletter, there are many great ones to choose from. Here is a list of some of our favorites:

- www.constantcontact.com
- www.Aweber.com
- www.databack.com
- www.1shoppingcart.com
- www.icontact.com
- www.verticalresponse.com

Although the companies above represent the best in newsletter services, we do have a disclaimer to make. We have elected to use Constant Contact for the majority of our clients' newsletter strategy implementation. But we want to give you your choice to find the best services for your situation.

But now the responsibility comes down to you and no one else: How do you write it well?

The seven rules of authorship

Here are our rules for writing a newsletter, but they can also apply in large part to blog posts, articles, booklets, and so forth.

HIGHLIGHTS OF CHAD'S INTERVIEW WITH GAIL GOODMAN, CEO, CONSTANT CONTACT

Reprinted with permission of Gail Goodman ©2011. All rights reserved.

On branding: If you make small businesses successful, they stay a long time and tell their friends. The way we've grown our brand is through great customer experience and by putting our customer success before our success. They needed a little bit of know-how combined with coaching with a personal touch.

On innovation: We spend a lot of time understanding our customers' challenges. We don't think they are going to tell us what to build, but they are telling us what their problems, issues, and opportunities are. We layer on top of that a culture of continuous improvement and innovation.

On key mistakes customers make: They focus primarily on new customers vs. existing ones. Your current customers are your best channel to new customers and there is probably more business available from your current customers than you think; also, thinking that marketing is about promotion rather than engagement and informational content.

On social media: It's about customer and prospect engagement through the creation of an online dialog that then exposes you to their network and creates an implied endorsement. The voice you want to amplify is your customer's and not your own. The visibility for you is generated, not when your customers read you on social, but when they engage with you, which means they "like" you, connect, and share with you. That is when their customers see you.

Rule #1: Tell them what they need to know, not everything that you know

Most writing is far too prolix and verbosity has become endemic in our society. But less IS more in writing, so how do you control your propensity to open the verbal floodgates?

Put yourself in your readers' shoes. Ask what they would need to know on any given topic to be able to pragmatically apply useful techniques immediately. Newspaper articles are written in an "inverse pyramid" style, so that the most important information comes first, and the less important can always be edited out at the end for space limitations.

You have no such luxury in a newsletter that we're advocating be confined to about a screen or 800 words or so. (An average magazine page, without advertising, has about 800 words.) So ask yourself merely this: What are the three or four most vital points, and how can I express them without verbiage?

Which leads us to rule #2.

Rule #2: A picture is worth 1,000 words, but an example is worth 1,000 pictures

People relate best and most immediately to situations with which they are familiar and/or in which they've found themselves (or could readily imagine themselves). Consequently, using personal stories and examples to make your points will both dramatically shorten your article and bring life to it, as in the following example: "Have you ever been in a classroom where the professor tells you everything he or she ever learned but doesn't respond to a question and rarely looks up from the notes? How effective was that learning compared to the professor who wades through the room interacting?"

You've been there, and so have we, and you can see (visualize, remember) immediately what that was like and why the point is so valid. There's no need to try to translate a conceptual theme using thousands of words.

Try to describe a spiral staircase with your hands at your side. At best you'll say that it's a continuing 360-degree, ascending stair which revolves back upon its own central axis.

That's nowhere near as effective as saying, "Picture a corkscrew."

Rule #3: Don't use no bad grammar

Don't fall victim to the debasement of the linguistic currency.

The internet is largely informal, to the extent that you can readily find obscene and scatological references on Facebook and YouTube (which is the web at both its best and its worst in terms of what's posted there).

Keep your content civil and intelligent, as if you were conversing with acquaintances you've met, but not family or friends at a hockey game. You're not talking to insiders, but to those with whom you may do business some day. You don't want to offend, you want to impress.

If needed, find an editor or someone who will simply read your newsletter before publication for obvious errors. For example, the correct phrase is "between you and me," not "between you and I," even though the latter may seem more refined. You don't have to know that the reason behind the fact that "between" is a proposition, which takes the objective "me" and not the nominative "I," but you do have to get it right.

If your grammar isn't correct, and you're not smart enough to find someone to correct it, why would your products and services be any better?

Rule #4: Same place, same time

Newsletters, like advertising, depend on consistency as much as content. You need to have the publication distributed at the same time every month, or whatever your frequency is.

If you use a listserv like databack.com, that's easily programmed, but *you still have to plug in the content at the right time.* Place your distribution on your calendar (which is why the first of the month is so convenient and obvious), and write a few newsletters in advance so that there are always some "in the bank." That way a deadline is never threatening and, if you're like us at all, you may not produce your very best quality when you're up against an impending deadline.

You can always substitute a more timely article in your newsletter, but a "backup" comes in handy to maintain your distribution deadline, especially if you have a heavy travel schedule. (Of course, with the techniques and sites we've already mentioned, you can write and distribute an electronic newsletter no matter where you are in the world so long as there is web access.)

Rule #5: Stop, thief!

It's fine to publish something of someone else that's of interest to your readers, since your venue is going to derive value by being the medium for the message. But you can't have a useful, legitimate newsletter that simply consists of things others write and you steal, though many people try to do this.

They are as obvious as a ham sandwich.

There was a guy in Australia who simply took renowned consultant and author David Maister's blog and reprinted it, substituting his name for David's. So if David were in Sweden speaking about his book, this guy would simply print the blog item as if he were in Sweden speaking about a book! There is a guy who's written a book that's entirely plagiarized (other people's concepts and words) and on his websites he posts sayings from famous people—H. L. Mencken or Oscar Wilde—as if they're his own!

When you do find something useful you wish to reprint, run it as a guest column with the other person's name and contact information and copyright—and with their permission. If you're just quoting something brief but it belongs to someone else, then use this template:

- Name
- Source
- Link
- Copyright information
- The phrase "reprinted with permission"

That's the way you'd want to be treated.

Rule #6: Create analogies and metaphors

Above we said, "It's as obvious as a ham sandwich," which is a phrase Alan introduced into his writing years ago. That's an analogy (which uses "like" or "such as" for comparisons) and it captures attention.

What are the metaphors (representations) that will color and amplify your writing? "Put your own oxygen mask on first" (which the airlines implore in case of emergency) we use as a metaphor for taking care of yourself first and being comfortable with a healthy selfishness. Think about word constructions and verbal examples that will solidify your concepts *and cause memorable calls to action uniquely attributable to you*.

Don't merely talk about growth—cite "escape velocity." Put some thought into these and introduce those that you want to return to with the purpose of identifying them with your thought leadership and intellectual property.

Rule #7: Keep evolving while employing intelligent design

Consistency doesn't mean blandness, and discipline doesn't denote a rut. Our newsletters progressed from text to HTML, from small to large, from focused to more general, and so forth. Were these the causes or effects of our business growth and increasing diverse audience? Who can say and who cares?

You must evolve with the times and design approaches that thrust you to the leading edge. Don't merely be content because your subscriptions are moderately and continually growing, or a few people write in regularly to tell you how much they enjoy your newsletter. Keep shaking things up so that others are inclined to try you out and regular readers establish RSS feeds to be alerted every time you publish. Try a few special issues from time to time in addition to your regular schedule.

Never "sit by the incoming metrics" to see how many people unsubscribe! Your goal is high quality and provocation for your target audience, not to become a global newsletter subscription leader.

Write for your audience, expressing yourself and your values, and keep challenging them and yourself to be leaders in your chosen field. There's the best writing formula you can possibly have. Call it the Eleventh Commandment.

Dramatic subscription growth

There's nothing wrong with dramatic growth, however, you want it o]to be within your highest potential chosen audiences.

And you want those people to heed, to listen, to absorb. There's a great line from *The Navigator* by Morris West: "The trouble with the high place is that you don't know if it's the voice of God you hear or only the echo of your own mad shouting." Thus, if you're the only one reading and listening to yourself, you're just shouting in the wind.

By now, you should be convinced to implement an effective newsletter strategy or improve the one you have. Yet the most challenging part remaining is to find the people to send it to, who want to receive it, and to grow this list significantly. This last part of this chapter will focus exactly on that: how to establish and grow your list.

We do acknowledge that one of the objectives (definitely not the only one) of having a website is to attract visitors to register for your newsletter, and we therefore recommend you incorporate the ability to register on your home page, all your interior pages, blog, email signature, social media platforms, and when providing special incentives such as eBooks. Yet, until credibility and trust are established, or the visitors truly desire to receive an offer, the likelihood of someone subscribing is quite low.

The best practice is to let your potential subscribers do this themselves by using the opt-in method. Although we would never recommend you add "strangers" to your distribution list, we do however suggest you take a bit more "assertive" approach when you first start building your subscriber list. Why not add your clients, colleagues, partners, friends, family, and attendees at your speaking engagements?

Make sure it's easy to register for your newsletter. The visitor should not have to feel tricked or forced to give you their firstborn in return for your newsletter. Unless you have created a newsletter that you charge a fee for, the minimum requirement is the visitor's email address and perhaps their first name so you may address it properly when sending out your newsletter. If you feel it is necessary to capture additional marketing segmentation questions on the registration page, we recommend you make these additional entry fields optional, otherwise you will run the risk of turning the visitor away.

Below is an example of how Chad incorporates the registration to his newsletter in his email signature:

Subscribe to our *Raising The Barr* free monthly electronic newsletter, jammed with resources, articles, and tips on technology, business, and internet strategy: www.cbsoftware.com/cbnn/newsletter_signup.php

To read my latest article, "How to Monetize Your Website," click below: www.cbsoftware.com/cbnn/how-to-monetize-your-website.php

Virtual Reality

If people feel they are receiving value, they opt in. If they feel their email and contact information is going to be used and abused, they run away.

There are intrusive and nonintrusive ways of suggesting a visitor register for your newsletter. Figure 7.6 on page 156 is an example of a nonintrusive invitation to the newsletter. It is "softly" displayed on the screen.

A recent trend is showing an intrusive display that pops up a few seconds after you arrive to the site you are visiting. To determine what works best for your target audience, we recommend you try them both and measure the results for several months. See Figure 7.7 on page 157.

As we have suggested before, make it easy for subscribers to opt in or opt out. We recommend a single opt-in to make it easy for the subscriber and avoid the confirmation email sent to the subscriber being caught in anti-spam software. When and if the subscriber decides to stop receiving your newsletter and opt out, do not send them a

Figure 7.6: **Newsletter invitation**
Reprinted with permission of Kathy Kingston ©2011. All rights reserved.

confirmation email. We find this practice irritating as well as the practice that sends this person more bribery-type incentives to convince them to stay with you.

If you are able to create multiple newsletters that provide different value, consider offering different frequency and even registration opt-ins. See Alan's registration page in Figure 7.8 on page 158.

Let's talk about *auto-responders*. These are the emails that are sent out automatically after a purchase of one of your products such as a newsletter. Let us suggest that the most important one is the first automated email being sent out. The reason is that the subscriber just registered and is not already accustomed to your newsletters. Therefore,

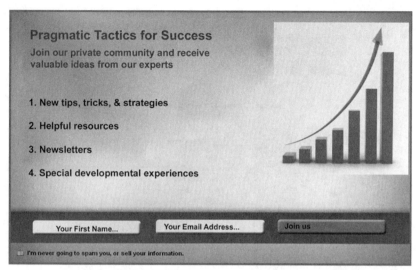

Figure 7.7: **Intrusive invitation**

why not formulate the first automated email response not just to thank the subscriber, but also offer them additional genuine value:

> *Thank you for joining my private subscriber community. You will receive ongoing articles, tips, and best practices. As my appreciation for you signing up, I am including a link to download our eBook,* The Bridge to Web Success, *as well as our video on 10 Newsletter Marketing Mistakes. I hope you enjoy this and find it to be of value, and please contact me if I can be of help.*
>
> *Best, Chad*

You may also consider sending out multiple emails that are staggered several days apart from each other, each one containing additional value and offerings.

Make sure that if the email recipient clicks on the reply option in their email, that it comes directly to you. We have seen too many irritating practices where recipients were unable to reply. This option either did not exist or was sent to a bogus email. *Make it easy for subscribers to get ahold of you!*

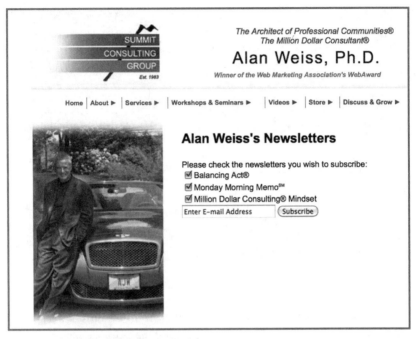

Figure 7.8: **Multiple subscription invitations**

We are not fans of the sales newsletter that in our minds resembles an infomercial. Among the key objectives we have when we deliver our speaking presentations are to deliver great value, engage the audience, create interest in contacting us, and to stay in touch with them. The best way to stay in touch is to add them to our newsletter distribution list. Here are the top three things we recommend:

· Offer them a special report during your presentation. "There are nine key mistakes entrepreneurs make when they develop their newsletter strategy. Let me share the top three mistakes right now, and for those of you interested in the entire white paper, email me directly or make sure to leave your business card with me."

· Similar to the previous example: "In a couple of minutes I will share with you the top nine mistakes entrepreneurs make. You probably want to have your pen and paper ready." Then share with them a link that takes them to a landing page offering this free resource where they have to register to get it.

· Let them know that you are working on a brand-new ebook and will be glad to make it available to this group upon completion.

Another effective way to increase your distribution list is to keep creating new offerings such as ebooks and other products. Once created, build a landing page that promotes this free ebook and "force" the user to submit their email address and first name in order to receive it. You may then create an attractive image, representing the ebook, that is then placed in the "What's New" section of the homepage, the margins of your interior pages, as well as your blog, email signature, and social media profiles. The example in Figure 7.9 illustrates such landing page promotion of an ebook. Also, instead of the ebook, you may consider placing a video that will present you discussing the benefits of the products, and offering additional incentives.

As far as the placement of your promotion in your newsletter, we recommend you place this in the margins, between articles, and at the end. The major learning point here is that you need to "softly" embed such among great value.

Additional secrets and best practices:

· One of the most successful promotions we send out are "Alan's Developmental Experiences" emails that are distributed once or twice per month. These, usually, are simple text emails that alert the subscribers to new experiences. Although we recognize that we don't know where our next hit comes from, we do know that this email in conjunction with everything else we do is very effective.

· Anytime you are asked to be interviewed by others, you must agree to do so. This will expose you further to others and will give you the opportunity to inject gentle promotions (seeding)

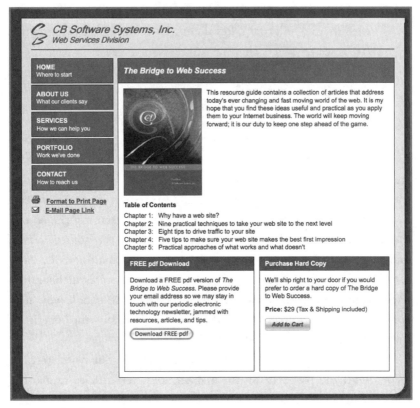

Figure 7.9: **ebook promotion**

while answering your interviewer's questions and delivering value.

· Suggest to others that they interview you, which makes sense anytime you provide value to their target audience.

· Interview others and especially thought leaders and popular bloggers. This will provide value to your audience and most likely will be featured on their sites and blogs, therefore promoting you as well.

· Promote your podcasts and videos on your site, blog, iTunes, and YouTube, and include the link to email registration as well as the incentive products.

- Become active on others' blogs and online forums and shame-lessly promote yourself while becoming genuinely provocative as a thought leader.
- Partner with others and make a "special" offer that can be sent via email, newsletter, or video. Your colleague will then send this special promotion to their list, genuinely promoting you, or you may do the same for them. This special offer takes the person to the free offer's landing page, where they need to register to get it.
- Several of our clients have been successful in purchasing a targeted database list and then sending its members powerful offers. If you have a very clear target audience, you can purchase names for as little as a few cents a name. Our colleague in Aus-tralia, Rob Nixon, has been brilliant attracting accountants—his specialty—to his periodicals. But you must be careful about spam laws, as Rob would be the first to tell you.

The key to establishing and growing your database is to nurture it. To do so effectively, you must be assertive and vigilant about consistent, powerful value created and sent to your audience. Consider every contact and every person who approaches you a potential name for your database and subscriptions.

After all, if you truly believe in the value you're bringing, then you're doing them a favor.

Myths and Monsters

how to be effective by ignoring conventional wisdom

 Strange sounds

It was one of those sleepless nights for Chad, 2 A.M., when he decided to surf the net and review a site of a prospect. Not realizing that his teenage son was on his computer earlier and had the speakers turned all the way up, Chad launched the site and almost had a heart attack. His speakers, previously set by his son to the maximum possible, blasted some commercial-like music played from the homepage of that site. The whole house shook while his family quickly awoke with fear of a rare local earthquake.

This story obviously serves to illustrate our point about intrusive sounds, but does your site have such sounds that play when the visitor reaches your pages?

We would first ask, what is the true purpose of such music and sound, and how does it benefit the visitor? Assuming you have a convincing answer, we would then question why it plays automatically and intrusively, which could only serve to irritate and not add value. So if music or sounds are available on your site, let your visitors have the control whether they want to play them or not. This chapter will focus on discussing irritating site traits, biggest mistakes, myths, and some of the worst practices.

Virtual Reality

Your site should entice with value rapidly, not pretend to be an amusement park or fun house.

Allow us please to vent a bit more, but without music for the moment: The next annoying issue are the videos that pop up and start playing automatically. If your site has them, we acknowledge that you probably worked hard at creating them, you are excited about having them viewed by others, and you were probably advised that unless you have them start playing automatically, visitors will not click to play them.

If so, we recommend you reconsider this strategy. As a visitor, when we arrive at your site, we are looking for something interesting to read, listen to, or watch. We know what a video looks like, and if we want to watch it, we will click on it. Otherwise, you run the risk of irritating the visitor, especially when this video keeps playing each time the visitor displays this page.

Next are the sites that flash a pop-up in your face to invite you to chat online with someone at the other end. Since we are all about providing pragmatic options, we do acknowledge that the option itself is a good alternative to provide to your visitors, especially when they feel they have additional questions while surfing your site. However, the issue we have with this is with its intrusiveness, and not the solution itself. Figure 8.1 shows an example of a solution from LivePerson (www.

Figure 8.1: An offer to interact

LivePerson.com), which enables your site to interface with such online help.

We are sure you can tell by now that we are not fans of intrusive pop-up or pop-under techniques. They are irritating, presumptuous, redundant, betray our trust, and take away our control as visitors. Another such technique already discussed in Chapter 7 is the email registration invitation. Figure 8.2 on page 166 is an example of such an invitation that pops up on the site as soon as you arrive. The first button we usually look to click on is the close button or the previous page button to get us out of there as quickly as possible.

It comes as no surprise that one of the configuration options in our browser setting is *to block pop-up windows*. More internet service providers have blocked such options on their servers, although certain online marketers are still inventing more such techniques, as they have nothing better to do with their time. Sites that display advertising in the middle of the page that forces you to close that window, sites that prevent you from navigating back by disabling the back button, and

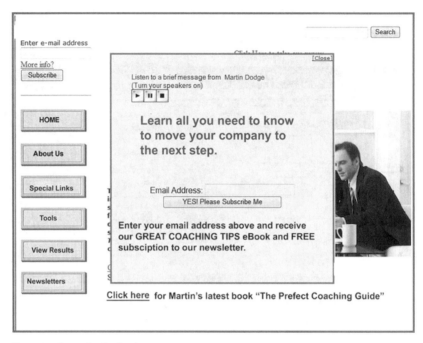

Figure 8.2: **Intrusive invitation**

sites that disable the ability to close your browser are those we find to be despicable attempts to turn visitors off and guarantee they never come back through overly aggressive marketing—if you can even call these devices "marketing."

Navigating your site should not feel like strolling in the local zoo, where every corner may yield a different, unexpected, and perhaps even scary sound (or unpleasant odor).

The key here is to put yourself in your visitors' shoes and understand that you only have one opportunity for a first impression.

When you build your site, have someone test it in beta version. Have people you trust "shop the site," and obtain objective feedback. It's hard to proofread something you've written yourself, and similarly, it's hard to test something you've created yourself (including working closely with your web designer).

CASE STUDY
The Floating Head

An individual Alan was coaching invited him to view his newest website. The landing page was a blue sky, with the site owner's head floating around it (you can't make this stuff up). Alan couldn't figure out how to navigate from there, so he gave up and called his client.

"Don't you get it? You have to click on my head!" he explained proudly.

"Is this a business website or an arcade game?" asked Alan.

The client was indignant, citing the time and expense invested to create the effect. But that's the problem when we simply choose to satisfy our own egos and not think about the client or customer and their best interests.

Ask yourself how quickly the visitor can arrive at your value for him or her, and what supports and speeds that journey, versus what impedes and slows it. Odds are, random sounds and strange encounters are not going to help anyone understand you any better or any faster.

The twilight zone

Let's review the top website myths right now.

I've been successful without a website

Imagine how much more successful you may become with an effective website. Your customers expect you to have one, and not having one is negligent in today's competitive electronic economy.

Creating a site would guarantee that visitors will show up

To do so takes hard work, marketing, commitment, patience, consistency, delivering value, and creating relationships. Quality trumps quantity.

You need to optimize your homepage for search engines such as Google

The truth is that you should first optimize your site for *human beings*, and then for search engines. The second reality check is that when optimizing your site (Chapter 9 will get into this), you need to focus on primarily optimizing your interior or landing pages rather than the homepage. Otherwise, your visitor, when arriving to the homepage, has to figure out where to go from there.

Placing products on your site will immediately increase your sales funnel and revenues

We highly recommend the placement of products as we have discussed when covering the marketing gravity and accelerant curve topics. It takes marketing commitment, brand recognition, and multiple marketing channels to get people to purchase your products. You're better off with a few high-quality offerings than a plethora of junk.

I am not a techie and this is all way too complicated

Technology has become easier than ever, facilitating tasks such as creating and posting content. Not only should you dive in and do it but hiring an expert to spend a short time with you will enable you to get up and running rather quickly.

I should take on the responsibilities of designing, coding, and sustaining my websites

Although there are many tasks we recommend you learn how to quickly do yourself, for the same reasons your clients should hire you, we recommend you hire true experts to help you avoid the traps, take advantage of the most powerful and effective technologies, and help you accelerate your success. Besides, your time is more valuable focusing on your areas of expertise and helping your clients.

I need to share everything I know and my methodologies

Visitors want succinct information to help improve their condition. They could care less about methodologies. Demonstrate "what" is important more than "how," and offer diagnostics whereby they can assess where they are and where they ought to be.

The more hits the better

The key is creating credibility and quality relationships with customers and not focus on meaningless hits. Five thousand hits a day from irrelevant people are worthless. (Remember all the spam you get in foreign languages!?)

It's all about the technology

We actually believe that the business strategy comes first and technology is the great enabler to help complement and execute the strategy.

I can't develop my own content

As previously indicated, there are many ways to develop content and there should be no excuses to not develop it. We've explained in Chapters 1, 4, and 7 how to create and constantly repurpose and recyle.

Global is too global

You have to start thinking big and leverage your efforts to reach out to larger audiences. As one of our enthusiastic clients stated at a meeting, "Global isn't big enough for us!"

Key website mistakes redux

- *Thinking that the visitor cares about you.* Recognize they don't and they only care about the value provided to them.
- *Site is ineffective and nonengaging.* Reduce redundancy of content, write in a pithy and succinct style, incorporate dynamic diagnostic tools, videos, and surveys, and make it interesting and intriguing for visitors to click on.
- *The site lacks trust and credibility.* Add testimonials, showcase clients, results, and your provocative intellectual property.

- *The site uses Flash extensively and intrusive pop-up windows.* Avoid these and replace them with effective and pragmatic concepts (discussed in previous chapters).
- *Not publishing regularly enough.* No one knows about you. Therefore, publish prolifically, learn to market effectively, and promote yourself shamelessly.
- *The content is stagnant.* Innovate, reinvent, and repurpose content.
- *Moving pages elsewhere.* If you must do this, make sure you create a redirect from the old page to the new one.
- *The site looks tacky and amateurish.* Hire an expert to help you become world-class.
- *The visitor cannot quickly figure out what your focus is all about.* Develop a strong value proposition and clear essence of what it is you do.
- *The site contains broken links.* Test your site thoroughly and often.
- *The site is slow to load.* This usually is due to poor and heavy use of images that are too large to load quickly. The other typical reason is that the server where your site is hosted is too slow, with too many sites hosted on it.
- *Stranding visitors on a page with no back navigation.* When opening a new browser window upon clicking on a link within your site domain, people should be able to retain context and connections with where they've recently been.
- *Finding out who you are is either impossible or professional, biographical information is nonexistent.* Make sure your bio is easily found.
- *It is impossible to find an easy way to contact you.* Make your phone number and email easily accessible from ALL site pages, as well as your contact page. Some sites guard against spam so aggressively that they also guard against prospects' contacts.
- *Not responding quickly to inquiries and comments.* Monitor this daily; make it a standard to reply within 24 hours, no matter where you are.

Downloads vs. avalanches

Chad recently returned from a speaking engagement where he presented to the Connecticut National Speakers Association (NSA) chapter. While arriving at the airport for the flight back home, he decided to quickly check email. He used his iPhone and a personal hotspot connection (very cool technology), which provides several devices with complete connectivity to the internet.

He opened his iPad, which immediately connected to his personal network, and noticed an email from a trusted colleague suggesting he check out an interesting site. Having only a few minutes to spare, he clicked the link, which launched a browser, and found a well-designed page, loaded with provocative and intriguing titles to explore.

One immediately grabbed his attention. He clicked on the title and the dialog box came up alerting him that the file download has just started and would take approximately 45 minutes to complete.

How aggravating is this?

We often create the functionality of allowing visitors to our sites and our clients' sites to download a variety of file types, to provide them with options for additional and easier future access to such files. Here are some reasons and the file types we provide for such download options:

- Make your booklet available as a PDF.
- Make your podcast audio recording available as an MP3 file, which can be easily placed on an iPod or similar device to play.
- Make your video available as an MP4 (other video formats are available) file, which will enable visitors to play it on their iPads or any mobile device at their leisure, without the need to be connected to the internet.
- Provide your how-to checklists in spreadsheet format, which will enable the visitor to quickly put them into action.
- Enable your documentation to be downloaded as a text file that will give the visitor the ability to modify and personalize it.

- Make a copy of your PowerPoint (Microsoft) or Keynote (Mac) presentation and allow your visitors to download it so they may better internalize your presentation. Also, why not convert your presentation to a PDF document?
- Make your text articles available both as HTML pages for quick and instant access as well as PDF so visitors may archive them for future access.

Assuming you do or are going to provide such download options on your site, which we urge you to do, we then recommend that you let the visitor know that they are about to click on a download link

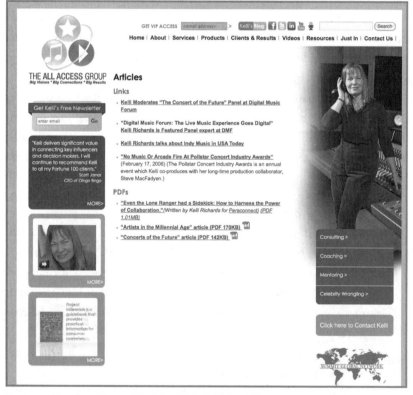

Figure 8.3: Alerting visitors about the file's download size

Reprinted with permission of Kelli Richards ©2011. All rights reserved.

and notify them about the type and size of that file (see Figure 8.3). The best way to do so is to incorporate the logo image of the file type (Adobe Acrobat for PDF, Microsoft Excel, and others) next to the title and in parentheses include the type and size. No surprises, please—you will make your visitors happier.

CASE STUDY
Kelli Richards on Leveraging

The ability to harness and leverage the internet has been absolutely pivotal to my success in business. It's without a doubt a necessary business partner for anyone who is self-employed. It provides a means of letting the world know you're out there ("hanging a shingle," as it were), a way to market your business, a way to handle lead-generation in sourcing clients, ties to your social media activities, and a means of engaging in direct e-commerce with your customers.

I've used it in all of these ways over the years. The way it works most commonly these days is that someone will reach out to me via LinkedIn (or vice versa) to explore the possibility of doing business together. They will be able to get a quick overview about me, what I do, my work and educational history, and select testimonials from colleagues. From there, they may be encouraged to visit my website where they'll get additional information about who I work with, what I've done, and how best to engage with me—all of which should provide them with ample credibility to gauge whether we should be pursuing collaborative opportunities together.

In turn I use the internet extensively to both conduct quick (or more thorough) research on who I may want to do business with, and get insights about their backgrounds and philosophies that will prove useful when we engage in direct conversation—and hopefully forge a mutually beneficial working relationship together.

An example of how this works is that I was recently contacted by Irene Cara, an award-winning singer, songwriter, actress, producer, and philanthropist of global stature and acclaim. She found me via the internet and was able to do enough research through my website to convince her that I may be

CASE STUDY, continued

able to assist her with this next phase of her professional growth and to help her mine opportunities for exposure and revenue in both the traditional and the digital world. She has since become a client, and we're creating some amazing results together—all virtually.

I honestly don't believe I could have achieved the level of success I have in running my own business without the internet—and would still be tethered to a traditional job—if it weren't for the ability to mine the power of the internet, and to engage people around the globe instantly.

—Kelli Richards, President and CEO,

The All Access Group, LLC, www.allaccessgroup.com

Reprinted with permission of Kelli Richards ©2011. All rights reserved.

Internet access speed is getting increasingly faster, yet we must recognize that when visitors arrive at our sites, there are several factors affecting their response time:

- The power and capacity of the server where your site is hosted.
- The number of sites hosted on that server.
- The number of users connected to that server.
- The type of applications being processed at that time.
- The internet speed or bandwidth that server is connected to.
- The size of files to download.
- The visitor's computer or mobile device capacity and bandwidth.

Since you have some control over the first six, by virtue of selecting the proper hosting partner for your site, we urge that you keep these items in consideration since the objective is to make these files easily downloadable. Have a discussion with your web and hosting partner to determine your best options and to optimize as much as possible the size of the files you provide for downloads.

The type of files provided for download should be universally accessible and not require special programs to open. However, why not make it easy for visitors to download the player that opens up the download file in case they do not have it on their computer?

For example, providing the ability to download Adobe Acrobat Reader on pages that have PDF files improves the visitor experience. Video files come in various formats such as: MP4, MOV, AVI, WMV, FLV, and others. You have several player choices such as Windows Media player or Quicktime, among others. Again, this discussion needs to take place with your web partner to make sure your visitors find the experience smooth and easy.

When visitors access your site from someone else's computer, they are dependent on the setting and configuration of that computer. This dependency is common when accessing a computer in a library, hotel, airport kiosk, or someone's private computer. It is then possible that the computer may not be able to download a PDF file or an audio or video file. We recommend that you make your files accessible to be viewed and played *inside your browser* in addition to the download options.

Playing audio and video files can be provided by streaming the files, which means that your site incorporates the ability to play such files instantaneously inside your browser without the need to download them. You can easily stream your videos by embedding YouTube on your site, and if you have a WordPress-powered site, incorporate the plug-ins mentioned earlier for playing the audio podcasts. Another great example is Alan's Friday Wrap,™ which is a subscription-based site we have created to provide paid subscribers with the ability to listen and watch Alan's audios and videos.

We add one new audio each Friday and one new video at the end of each month. Notice in the screenshot in Figure 8.4 on page 176 how we use Audio Acrobat (www.AudioAcrobat.com) to stream the files (audio and video) as well as the ability to download them.

The reason you want to provide visitors with the ability to download the files is to provide them flexibility, options, and convenience. This enables them to place the files on their personal electronic devices (e.g.,

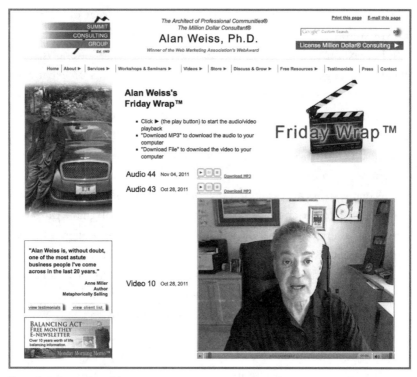

Figure 8.4: **Streaming video**

iPad, iPod, iPhone, and such) so they can listen and play them in their homes, in cars or on airplanes, or even while working out.

How is that for providing your knowledge repository ubiquitously and on the go?

One of the methods of sending files is as an attachment via emails. However, this method is best used for small files, probably less than 5MB, and we recommend using a web service to enable visitors to retrieve your files.

For the purpose of sending large files to clients we recommend using www.SendSpace.com or www.YouSendIt.com, which are both great for such tasks (see Figure8.5). This method should be considered instead of email when you need to send private and large files to your clients.

Say you're sending out a teleseminar audio recording as an MP3 download. We recommend the paid option, which is quite low ($8 per month for the entry level) and allows large files to be sent. Once you upload your file to this service, you are given a unique and private URL that can then be sent via email, or displayed at the end of the shopping cart when the visitor purchases a digital product. You may also brand your page to provide the user with the link for the download.

The application www.DropBox.com is one of the greatest recent inventions. It enables the setup of folders on the web, which reside in the cloud and are completely synchronized with all your devices such as computers, laptops, and mobile devices. The beauty is that you may work on a document on your desktop at home, save it to your DropBox-designated folder, which not only saves it to your local device, but synchronizes it with the cloud version.

As soon as you access your other devices such as your laptop, it will receive the document from the cloud and synchronize and place it on that laptop. You then have the flexibility of working on that document on your plane ride, save it on your laptop, and as soon as you connect to the internet, it synchronizes it with the cloud and then your other

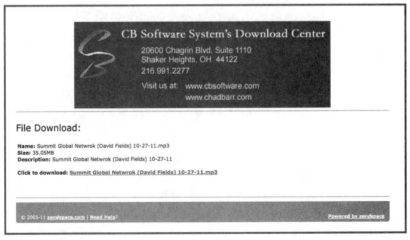

Figure 8.5: **Using SendSpace.com for large files**

CASE STUDY
Wrong Turns: Chad's Dilemma

I recently decided to contact AT&T Wireless and inquire about using them as my mobile phone carrier. I figured that today, with the awesome power of the internet, I should be able to retrieve their phone number rather quickly. With my browser launched and Google ready to accept my search criteria, I quickly typed "AT&T" and then clicked on the first link provided as the search result. Their home page came up rather quickly, but to my surprise (perhaps not) I was unable to find a phone number to contact so I may hopefully then get connected to a human voice. Being the resilient and the web-astute individual that I am, I was not ready to give up yet, so I found myself still looking all over the page. After several minutes of searching, I finally found the "Contact Us" option buried in tiny type all the way at the bottom of the page.

One may think that the obvious words "Contact Us" should quickly reveal the hidden phone number I was so desperately seeking. "But NO!" as Steve Martin used to humorously pronounce on the *Saturday Night Live* show. I then had to type my answers to more interrogation-like questions so I may perhaps be given the coveted phone number.

If I ever wondered how exhilarated Columbus might have felt when he finally discovered that piece of land, I now knew. The phone number was finally displayed on my screen. I quickly grabbed my pen and jotted down the number to make sure that I would not have to go through similar suffering in the future. I guess it must have been my voice, when to my great surprise I heard the words "Sign me up" come out of my mouth and the happy AT&T representative did just that.

I must also admit that navigating their site is like putting together the pieces of a puzzle blindfolded. We are not here to promote AT&T and have no financial interest in mentioning them here, yet we wanted to share this experience with you in order to cement our point. As you can see, it is critical that you make your visitor's information-retrieval experience quick and efficient so they don't take the wrong turn and exit your site forever.

devices. We often share certain folders with our clients to easily share and synchronize documents.

Does your site allow for streaming, or smooth download option, or does it create the avalanche effect? We've tried to show the difference between a roaring avalanche of uncoordinated and difficult access and an intelligent strategy for assisting visitors to access your intellectual property and your value to them.

One of the more irritating mistakes is the "broken link syndrome." Your visitor arrives at a page on your site, intrigued perhaps to click on a link to display the article they've selected, or to register for one of your events, and—oh no, the page is not found! This is known as the "broken link 404 page not found error." The simple solution is to make sure your site is well-tested by your web partner and you. However, we

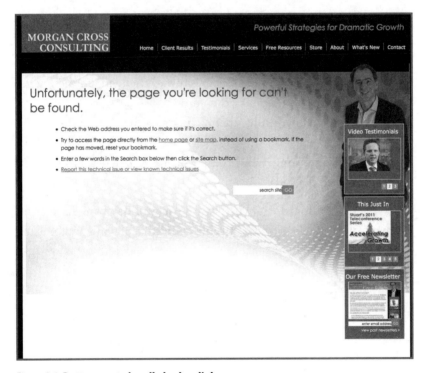

Figure 8.6: **Better way to handle broken link**
Reprinted with permission of Stuart Cross ©2011. All rights reserved.

do acknowledge that such mistakes unfortunately happen, and our solution is simple and elegant. Have your site coded in such a way that if a 404 page not found error is detected, your site will then display a friendly "page not found" page that is branded within the colors and template of your site design. Apologize to the visitor and provide them with options to contact you, search your site, or access the site map.

We also suggest you use tools on the web that can run through your site diagnostically to detect any broken links. One such tool is found here: http://validator.w3.org/checklink.

Imagine arriving at one of your favorite stores only to find a sign that says: "Under Construction." The equivalent on the web is not that much different. *We've seen both sites and pages that claim to be under construction for years!* What kind of message does that project to the client or prospect arriving at such pages? Negligence and laziness is our answer. When approached with such a dilemma, you have two options and here are our recommendations:

- Remove such pages from your site and then launch them when the content is ready for prime time.
- Create anticipation by committing to a live date and then display a message on the page such as: "We are excited to release this new section on xx/xx/xx," which is a date perhaps 60 or 90 days into the future.

Never, ever mislead your visitor with tricky or deceiving navigation. As mentioned previously, we've seen the practice of some web masters

Virtual Reality

If the store shelves are bare or broken, people won't shop, won't return, and will tell others not to go there, even if the place is spruced up later.

attempting to "lock" the visitor into the site and other practices that make you think you are being directed to a legitimate page only to find out you are not. This will ruin your credibility and assure the visitor is unlikely to come back, and even worse, they may warn others.

There are also the innocent and amateurish misleading navigation mistakes. Examples of such are images that seem clickable, yet when you hover your mouse over them you then discover they are not, or highlighted text in different font and colors that make you think it is a clickable link. The cardinal rule that should never be broken is *never underline text that is not a clickable hyperlink. It is amateurish and annoying.*

We've also seen too many sites with distracting, amateurish, and tacky images. Therefore, we recommend professional action shots representing you with your clients or partners, or showing you receiving awards and honors. These images, if used well, demonstrate credibility and help strengthen your brand. If you decided to select images that have been legally purchased from such services, we recommend your designer modify them by adding visual distortion or color gradient effect to make them unique. See the example in Figure 8.7. Demonstrating such planned color gradient effect in the bottom left, "Services" section.

There is far too much amateur use of language, silly use of emoticons (those silly smiley icons), and text shortcuts in professional writing on the web. Another serious deadly sin that is sure to "force" the visitor to take the wrong turn is the use of improper or poor language on one's site. We have seen a recent trend where some successful so-called "thought leaders" and internet marketers not only dumb down their language but also use profanity, such as the one seen by Tony Robbins on www.Ted.com, apparently thinking he may be effective or "cool." If you are thinking of doing so, don't! And if you are doing so, stop it! It does not position you as authentic, transparent, or cool. On the contrary, the use of profanity, obscenity, and scatological references are the signs of someone who is intellectually bereft and witless. Those references indicate an absence of intellectual heft and a disrespect for

Figure 8.7: **An example of color gradient effect, bottom left**
Reprinted with permission of Libby Wagner ©2011. All rights reserved.

one's audience. That's not exactly going to empower you to dominate the web.

As we indicated earlier, browser optimization and compatibility is critical to make sure that your site displays properly in all of the top and popular browsers as well as mobile devices. Since this also pertains to this section, let us suggest that unless your site is properly optimized, it is then likely to be out of kilter, which means navigation will not display and act properly, images and text will not display as intended, and visitors are sure to get confused and go elsewhere accidentally (or deliberately!).

Another popular mistake is long and nested dropdown navigation menu options. When it comes to nested navigation, our preference

Figure 8.8: **Effective "nesting"**
Reprinted with permission of Omar Khan ©2011. All rights reserved.

is to not exceed more than two levels. Notice in the example above how we have the four options under "Services" and we then nested three additional options under "Leadership for Change." We have also included the triangle symbol to signify this.

Other elements that quickly influence the visitor to stay or exit your site are design, organization, colors, and fonts. Keep your pages clutter-free and remember that less is more with fewer elements on each page. Reduce the text to a bare minimum on your homepage. We suggest you give consideration to the number of colors and font types in your design and implementation. Font colors should be in contrast to the background colors so they stand out and don't get washed out by the background: 20- to 22-point fonts work great for headings, 16- to 17-point fonts work great for subheadings, and 12- to 13-point fonts are good for text. *Web-friendly fonts such as Verdana and Arial are ideal, as they will render the same in all browsers.*

The inclusion of a link to your sitemap on all pages makes it easier for both your visitors and search engines to find the content, and eliminates the need to include text navigation on the bottom of the pages, as was customary years ago. One additional consideration is to enable navigation to the previous or next page within a menu section. For example, say that under "Services," one of the options is "Mentoring," which contains three options such as "Private Roster," "Guided Program," and "Total Immersion." To make it easier to navigate, you may want to include the previous or next option with these three options or display the three navigation options on each of the pages.

Just as the invention of the compass helped sailors navigate the seas, today's global positioning system (GPS) is a lifesaver but also a matter of great convenience for all of us. Therefore, we encourage you to implement your own version of a compass or a GPS on your site for your visitors to use. A search box that allows the internal search of your content will just do that trick. And if all else fails, they can always pick up the phone and call or email you.

You did place that information on all pages, right?

CHAPTER 9

You're Going to Optimize My What?

how to really gain web torque and horsepower

Search engine torque

Several years ago, a prospective client contacted us to inquire about a piece of software we had developed. When I inquired how he found us, he said, "I searched for the words *autoquotes integration* and you came up right at the top." (See Figure 9.1 on page 186.) This inquiry eventually led to a six-figure project for us. We are not here to boast; rather, we'd like to share with you that search engine marketing (SEM) does represent one of the spokes in our internet marketing gravity wheel, as discussed in prior chapters. And before you fully commit to it, you had better read the next paragraph.

What we are about to share with you may disturb some, especially the experts, and may be a relief to others. Let us present you with a hypothetical, yet realistic, case scenario.

Figure 9.1: **Googling for information**

Say you are a consultant who focuses on strategy work, you are located in New York, and you are hoping to leverage search engines, such as Google, to bring traffic to your site and inquiries from potential buyers. When researching Google's global monthly results (go to www.google.com/AdWords and then click on "get keyword ideas") showing how many people search for such terms, here is what we quickly found: 60,500 searches for "strategy consultants," 33,100 for "strategic consultants" and 260 for "strategy consultants New York" (see Figure 9.2).

Although the number of searches looks somewhat intriguing, here are our contrarian viewpoints:

· Who makes up these search numbers? Is it you, your colleagues, competitors, journalists, students, researchers, internet search consultants, others, or your actual potential buyers?

· What is the percentage of actual buyers who are really represented in these numbers?

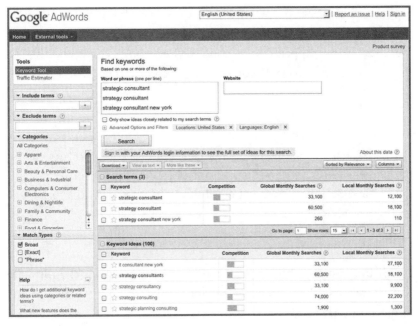

Figure 9.2: **Keyword search**

- Do you think your buyers are searching for you online in order to purchase your products and services?
- What is the likelihood that your target buyer is actually using the keyword or phrase that you think they would use?
- Who should we actually write for? Should your content focus on effective writing for people or search engines?

Our position is that corporate buyers (in the wholesale business model) are not searching the web for entrepreneurs and service organizations such as ours to hire. The key is referrals, effective marketing gravity, and building trusting relationships. We do, however, acknowledge that consumers (the retail market) may be searching for products and services, and therefore search engines do play a stronger role there.

Now, the important question: How many strategy consultants exist worldwide? Say the number is 10,000. What if 5 percent of them have optimized their site properly? That means that 500 would compete to be displayed on the first page. Since Google typically displays 10 results per page, if you happen to be among the lucky ones, you would then be placed on the first page. If not, you might be placed on page 50!

Virtual Reality

Search engine optimization (SEO) is WAY overrated because very few buyers troll the web to find your particular products and services. You're better off attracting prospects to your own sites yourself.

If by now you still want to continue your quest for the ultimate search results, then keep on reading. But first, let's clarify some important terms and concepts.

- *Search engine marketing* (SEM) incorporates the concepts used to leverage the power of various search engines to promote your site and effectively drive traffic to your various targeted pages.
- *Search engine optimization* (SEO) incorporates utilization of methods such as keywords, site ranking, and links to leverage your content in order to position your site higher in search results to attract more quality visitors.
- *Organic results* are the addresses (URLs) displayed as the result of your query that are not marked as ad results. It is most coveted to be listed on the first page of Google's search results and especially as the top three results. These results are served genuinely by Google and are not influenced by payments.
- *Paid results* are the addresses (URLs) displayed as the result of your query that are marked as ad results. These typically are listed on the right side of the browser and a few at the top. To be listed under ad results, you must pay and bid your way to the top. The more you pay, the higher the listing. If you desire to

be listed at the top, you must be the highest bidder. However, it may be acceptable and desirable for you to be listed as the third paid advertising, which means that you only have to overbid the current third position.

Interesting statistics we've seen fluctuating over the years indicate that 80 percent of clicks are given to the organic results, which are interpreted as much more credible, and 20 perent to the paid results. Think about your own online searching style and habits. What do you typically search for, and how? Once you are served the search results, do you focus only on a few organic results at the top, or explore the entire page? Do you view additional organic results on additional pages? Do you click on the sponsored ads?

Your answer should determine where you should invest your resources. Traffic to your site comes from many sources, such as when the visitor:

· Enters your site address (URL) into their browser.
· Enters the web page address (URL) that was shared with them (through other marketing efforts) into their browser.
· Enters your site address into their browser when receiving your company's paperwork such as invoice, purchase order, check.
· Clicks on your email signature links.
· Reads your newsletter and clicks on one of the links.
· Views your blog or site and clicks on links.
· Reads your guest contributor content, such as your article or your column on someone else's site, and then clicks on a link.
· Views your video on YouTube and clicks on the links to your site in the description area.
· Listens to your podcast on iTunes and clicks on the link to your site.
· Reviews your social media profile or content and clicks on the link.
· Sees your answer on LinkedIn and finds it interesting and clicks on your profile name.

- Finds interesting links on social bookmarking sites and clicks on one of yours.
- Finds your book on Amazon and clicks on the link to your site.
- Reads your article in article directories or an online community.
- Finds you on one of the trade associations to which you belong.
- Sees your comment on a blog and clicks on your link.
- Notices your press release and clicks on a link.
- Clicks on one of your banner ads or affiliate links.
- Is encouraged to bookmark your site for private use or for social media sharing.
- Uses search engines and clicks on the organic results.
- Uses search engines and clicks on the paid results.
- Uses Facebook paid advertising and clicks on the link to your landing page.

There are many companies attempting to provide search engine results, and as of May 2011, according to ComScore (www.comscore.com), the top three search engines were Google (65.5 percent), Yahoo (15.9 percent), and Microsoft (14.1 percent), which leaves the rest at less than 5 percent. We have seen some other statistics ranking Google at owning close to 80 percent of internet searches, which obviously positions them as the top search engine.

Recent studies are showing that the top three search platforms are Google, YouTube, and Facebook. Our position is, as of the writing of this book, unless you have large resources, including money, and depending on your target audience, if you decide to devote time, money, and energy, *focus your efforts on Google, YouTube, and Facebook.*

To avoid costly time and money mistakes, we recommend you retain a search engine advisor to help you implement the proper strategy.

The two most effective ways to improve your site's standing in search results are: First, develop great content in various formats such as articles, images, process visuals, podcasts, and videos. Second, attract links from other sites to your site. The most powerful ones are genuine and credible links from others and especially popular and powerful ranked sites such as *The Wall Street Journal*.

What should you optimize? Imagine searching for a key phrase and when clicking on the search results, you end up on the homepage of one site. You then need to start figuring out which site it is, how to navigate it, and find what you are looking for. Other items on that page most likely may also distract you. *The key to successful optimization is to understand that you are optimizing interior landing pages on your site, and not your homepage.*

For example, if one searches for "grow email distribution list," wouldn't it be nice if the search result takes you to the page containing the content with the answer to this question? See Figure 9.3, demonstrating how Google has picked up my blog article in the first search result position.

The search engine Holy Grail is obviously to be listed organically among the top three results of the first page. Your search engine marketing efforts should help you get there.

Figure 9.3: **Being found on a Google search**

Search horsepower

This section focuses on explaining some of the techniques and methodology for dealing with search engines with the best investment of your time for optimal results.

The job of search engines is to accurately index the web so that when a visitor enters a search query the search engine can accurately provide these results. In order to do so and throughout each day, software programs called "crawlers" or "spiders" search billions of connected pages to index them properly in their gigantic databases.

Over the years, these spiders have improved their algorithms to provide more accurate snapshots for each page on our dynamically changing web. Is it perfect? Far from it. But it is improving. What are the key components these spiders review and index? This glimpse into their logic will enable you to better understand what you should do to improve performance and accuracy so your buyers can better find you.

Identify your keywords—the words that help people find you

Here are ten ways to pinpoint keywords that will improve your rank in search results:

1. When you receive a web inquiry, ask visitors how they searched for you. Also ask this question for non-web inquiries.
2. Identify words and phrases that describe your company, products, services, and brands. If you were to search for your company, how would you do that?
3. Review your site analytics, which would reveal statistics regarding visits and sources.
4. Review Google's recommendations by visiting their AdWords page, and then clicking on "keyword ideas."
5. Learn from others by visiting the sites of your colleagues and competitors. View various pages and click on "view," and then click on "page source," which will identify the keywords used on these pages. Make a list of the ones that make the most sense for you.

6. Ask your clients and colleagues for their input on what would they be searching for if they were to search for you.

7. Keywords are unique to each of your pages. Each page should have a few unique words. For example, if you search "strategic profile," you will find 122 million results. Yet if you search for "internet strategic profile," there are 39 million results, and guess who is #1? The article we wrote on this topic which is found here: www.cbsoftware.com/cbnn/internet-strategic-profile.php.

8. The first few words should be the most highly focused on the page and strongly relate to the content on that page.

9. Incorporate your keywords in the content, but do not overdo it.

10. Keep your keywords relevant and simple. For example, rather than using "strategy," which garners in 639 million results, "strategy consultant" is a better choice that gets 1.5 million results. Yet, *"strategy consultant new york city" yields 26,100 results, which is even better optimization.*

Page titles (<title>) tags are critical, since they are the ones that are first displayed in the search results as well as at the top of your browser. Include your keywords in the page titles and make them reflective of your content, and provocative. We recommend you include your name or company name in the title, make it unique per page, and keep it within 70 characters.

Virtual Reality

With a relatively little time invested in the words you highlight and where they are placed, you can maximize the chances of people finding you quickly and emerge from the "noise" of the internet.

Although not used by the search engines for search results purposes, the meta description tag (<meta description>) is important since it is also displayed in the search results below the title. Keep it around 20 words.

Page headings should be provocative and when possible include the keywords.

When using images, name them with an "alt text" to improve the search engine association of that image to your content.

Web address format (URL) is important for its ranking by search engines. Incorporate as short and meaningful naming structures as you can, such as the article name divided by dashes. For example: www.YourDomain.com/search-engine-mistakes.

Incorporate a site map on your site, which then serves a double purpose: for visitors who are looking for a quick reference to find and navigate your content, and for search engines.

As mentioned previously, one of the most important concepts is to have links pointing to your site. Google gives much more credibility and weight for a link to your site coming from *The Wall Street Journal* than from your colleagues and friends who do not have such connections. Also, the use of anchor text is critical, so instead of creating a hyperlink with the words "click here" to point to one of your articles, it is far more effective and powerful to hyperlink the phrase: "nine key search engine mistakes" to the applicable article.

The secret to getting others to link to your site is to create powerful content and spread it virally so people are eager to share the links to your great content with others.

Now a few words on the practice of exchanging links. Although if done right and in a genuine way, Google will count it as a positive link to your site, we see such practices as a waste of time and energy that can be put into better marketing use, and we actually coined this practice as "reciprocal link grand theft." People seeking to do this usually have inferior sites and are trying to gain leverage from yours.

Another practice we loathe is that of submitting your site to services such as "link farms" that are supposed to provide your web address to hundreds or even thousands of sites they link to you. This again connects you with inferior locations. Beware of the abhorrent practice of creating fake blogs that automatically populate their content from others' blogs and then link that content to paid click services such as Google AdSense. These are nothing more than ad revenue gimmicks and can ruin you by association.

Since WordPress has become one of the most popular and robust development tools, it is also search-engine friendly. We recommend using a plug-in called "All in One SEO" which simplifies the optimization tasks and helps its overall optimization.

Google assigns a page rank to your site (0–10), which is their way of determining how important your site is. The higher the number, the higher the rank, yet we recommend you use that as a guideline rather than the score to your online success.

Let's now review what search-engine potholes to particularly avoid.

Search potholes

Let's explore some of the common search engine misconceptions and traps to avoid:

Trap: If a human can't figure out the context of the page, how would a crawler? Make sure your web page is clear to understand, visually and contextually. Don't overcomplicate it or load it with your complex methodology.

Myth: Stagnation of content on your website will hurt your ranking and web success. When reviewing sites visually and contextually, we've seen poor sites that are ranked highly and great sites that are ranked poorly. It should be obvious, though, that great content will attract more people to you, create a viral impact, enable search engines to index and find more of your content, and help position you as a thought leader.

Trap: Avoid creating "hidden" pages, which are not linked to and from other pages on your site. Although there may be logical reasons to do so at times, make sure all intended pages are easily navigated to and from other pages on your sites.

Myths: Meta tags are important for improved ranking and search engines finding you. This was true years ago *and is completely untrue now*. The only benefit is to display the text on the search results screen but it has no impact on its influence.

Trap: Not following the steps described in this chapter, such as paying attention to page titles, keywords, subordinate titles, and links. If you carry out the steps mentioned, not only will you avoid hurting your results, you will positively influence them.

Myth: Google page rank is accurate in demonstrating your search engine success. As we have indicated earlier, it is a guideline. We have seen sites with high Google ranking where the site owner is a starving artist and other sites with low page ranking representing the site of a world-class success. We have also seen results of searches displaying sites with low ranking at the top and above sites that are actually ranked higher. So ignore this. Yet, if you still prefer to check your own ranking and that of others, you may want to download and install the free Google toolbar found here: www.toolbar.google.com.

Trap: Thinking that all searches are equal and not realizing that individuals search differently and on various sophistication levels. Where this becomes a trap is in the mindset that your keywords should attract the perfect buyer, but they may not.

Myth: Thinking that there is a need to submit your site for acceptance by the search engines. This is old thinking and is unnecessary. A simple link to your site from any site will enable the search engines to find it and index it properly in their databases.

Trap: Spamming search engines for better placement. The most common mistake is to use the same keyword over and over on the same page, which is also known as "stuffing your keywords."

Especially ineffectual is the old technique of white type on a white background. This is a sure shot recipe to have your site banned or penalized by the search engines.

Myth: Optimizing the homepage instead of interior landing pages. As we have discussed earlier, you want to focus your attention on optimizing interior landing pages to achieve the best results.

Trap: Search engines cannot see your secured content, which usually resides behind passwords. Although this may be your intent, which is fine and correct, just keep this in mind to make sure you realize that search engines will not index such content.

Myth: Digital documents stored as PDF files are not seen and able to be indexed by search engines. This has changed and these documents are part of the indexed search engine databases.

Trap: Audio and video files cannot be indexed. Therefore, we recommend including short text attached to each, which highlights concepts represented in these files, for better search engine indexing and visitor experience.

Myth: The responsibility of improved search engine success lies entirely on the search engine algorithm. Actually, an even greater responsibility lies on you and your search engine partner or advisor.

Trap: Sticking to one proven methodology is the key. Google has the tendency to adjust their algorithms and therefore we recommend following the best writing and advice on this topic from us and other such professionals in order to spot and adjust to changing trends.

As you can imagine, the list can quickly get lengthier and even more technical. Since our approach is pragmatic, we suggest you always use common sense and this list as a quick reference point. Also keep watching our blogs www.contrarianconsulting.com and www.chadbarr.

com for changing trends and improvement suggestions on this and a variety of other topics.

From anonymity to client

You have heard us admonish, "You never know where the next hit comes from," which is quite applicable to concluding this chapter. What this statement means is that we are not always smart enough to be able to predict where our next customer will come from. We recommend that you engage in as many effective elements of marketing gravity as possible, such as soliciting referrals, commercially publishing your book, creating strong internet presence, speaking, nurturing your database, and other important elements covered thus far.

When a prospect becomes a customer, it is our prime opportunity to discover *what were the key reasons for becoming a customer* and we then must learn to use what we discover and continue these efforts. Unfortunately, too many of us focus on arbitrarily increasing hits to our sites rather than focusing on converting those hits to inquiries and actual business. A web troll recently boasted on Alan's blog of having more hits than Alan (which, actually, he did not), yet he also mentioned that he was not making much money!

Are you possibly losing sight of the forest for the trees or the trees for the leaves? We hope the following helps place this in the proper perspective.

Virtual Reality

You DO know what's worked for certain AFTER someone has become a client, IF you ask!

At his juncture, you may still be pondering whether site optimization is for you, or you are looking for additional ideas to implement in your search strategy. As we've indicated, we view search engine marketing as one of the spokes of the marketing gravity wheel, and before we share additional best practices with you, let us be contrarians for a moment longer.

Why stop now, right? Where would you say most of your business is coming from? Is it from existing or new customers? When it comes to our business and that of your clients, the answer is obvious—existing clients constitute the source of most of your business. Why, then, would you invest your limited resources on activities that are not directly connected to your existing customers who trust you? And we know that these customers are not searching for you on the web. *They already know you and trust you.* Of course, we all want to attract new customers, and we feel that there are more effective ways of doing so than desperately searching the search engines for them.

Rather than focusing on increasing traffic to your site, focus on converting that traffic to capturing their name and email addresses, inquiries, and business. Here is how you do that:

- Most people do not track whether their site is up and running all the time. Therefore, you must rely on a trusted hosting partner who makes sure your site is working 100 percent of the time. Otherwise, the likelihood of someone not being able to contact you or order your products and services is pretty high!
- Logic makes them think, emotion makes them buy. They are not buying your products or services, but the improvements your products and services have on their lives and businesses. Therefore, you need to engage the visitor emotionally. Acres of web real estate invested in text, background, "value," your "staff," and so forth, serve no purpose whatsoever. There is no emotional appeal. But testimonials, case studies, and typical client results that may strike someone's current "hot buttons" will cause a positive reaction.

- The stronger your brand, the stronger the conversion. Focus on strengthening your brand and credibility. Therefore, when someone searches for your type of offerings, when they find you and recognize your strong brand, they will then most likely purchase from you and not comparison shop.
- Increase the quality of leads by finding out how they discovered you and what they searched for. Once you find this out, adjust whatever is needed to maximize that attraction.
- Increase the trust factor by incorporating our ideas of how to establish credibility through testimonials, case studies, results, and so forth.
- Incorporate secured shopping for your purchasing, returns, and shipping policy.
- Incorporate flexibility of payments with options to accommodate the visitor's preference.
- Less is more. Be pithy and to the point.
- Make sure your site is fully compatible with all top browsers so all pages display as intended.
- Incorporate effective calls to action (e.g., "Enroll now!").
- Integrate with social media so visitors can track which of their friends may have engaged you before.
- Show the options and recommendations of what others benefited from or enjoyed.
- Provide easy accessibility to you personally and to additional information about contact methods.
- There is no bigger impact on conversion than creating an effective landing page. Figure 9.4 is an example of such a page, also found at www.doctorseibel.com/weight-control, incorporating videos and podcasts loaded with value where the objectives are to create the credibility to capture the visitor information or get them to contact you.

Once you have converted the visitors to prospects or clients, you must stay in touch with them and start nurturing the relationships

Figure 9.4: **An effective landing page**
Reprinted with permission of Dr. Mache Seibel ©2011. All rights reserved.

CASE STUDY
My Transition from the Silent Screen

I've been a physician and speaker for 30 years, been interviewed for radio and TV numerous times, and written and recorded award-winning songs. But during all that time my website was silent. When Chad suggested I make some videos for my website, I figured it would be a piece of cake. Stand up and shoot. Sit down and edit. Upload to the internet and spread the word.

It wasn't quite that easy. My first videos were mediocre; but with persistence, that changed and I'm now proud of my videos. These are some things that helped me in my transition from the silent screen.

The first thing I learned is that as a medical expert, I don't have to be an Academy Award-winning actor. It's not acting at all. I'm explaining things that

CASE STUDY, continued

I know really well. I got rid of the scripts and just talked about the topics I'm an expert in as if I were explaining it to a patient. The dialog changed from stiff to easy conversational. Placing a flip chart next to the camera with a few bullet points I wanted to cover made it natural and easy for me.

Clothes made a difference. I found ones that look good on camera. Some are too shiny; some don't fit as well; some cast a shadow on my neck. Experimenting with different wardrobes quickly made it clear which worked best.

I bought a Sennheiser ek 100 G2 lavaliere microphone for my lapel. It has a wireless transmitter that sends sound to a receiver that connects into the camera. This $500 investment made an enormous difference in sound quality.

The next step was thinking about who would be listening to my video. Although it might be thousands of people, they are not all in a large auditorium at the same time. Only one person on one computer screen is seeing me, which is like a personal conversation. I look right into the lens of the camera and have a conversation with one of my patients, only I speak as if the person is 10 feet behind the camera so that my voice seems confident and present. I keep reminding myself that there is a real person watching, so I stay as present and attentive to that lens as if the person were actually sitting in front of me.

My initial videos were long, 10 to 20 minutes. For some topics, that might work, but for health information, most people seemed to want very specific information in smaller bites. I now keep the videos on the short side and make each video very specific. My wife does the shooting and I ask how it sounded. If I wasn't in the moment, I just delete and reshoot. It saves a lot of time.

Once the basic information was flowing, I began to look for ways to fine-tune the video to make it even better. Watching my videos, I found that I had little mannerisms—my head moved a certain way, I rocked a little when I spoke, I blinked too much. I started practicing in the mirror. Knowing what to look for from earlier videos and practicing in the mirror helped me stop doing those things that I felt detracted from my presentation.

CASE STUDY, continued

I took voice lessons so my sentences would sound better and have more range and tonality. I try to continuously speak until I reach either a comma or a period in a sentence. Even though there is no script, talking this way took out the "uhmms" and the "so, uh's," etc. I found it is OK to pause for a thought. I didn't have to use a meaningless filler such as one of the ones just mentioned.

To make things go smoother, it's helpful to have a checklist: Make sure the wires are plugged in correctly, make sure the batteries are charged, turn off cell phones, place a sign on the door that you are "recording," have water available to stay hydrated, have extra light bulbs if you use lighting, etc. It's amazing the little things that can go wrong. It's amazing how many you can avoid with a simple checklist.

To learn editing, I bought a Mac and took lessons on iMovie at the Apple Store. This took some tenacity, and I just kept working on one video at a time until I could do it myself. As long as my content is accurate, I learned to live with minor imperfection, realizing that each video is a learning experience to make the next one better.

Give yourself three months and just go with the flow. It does keep getting better. Like learning to talk, one day you just start talking; and leave the silent screen behind.

—Mache Seibel, MD, www.DoctorSeibel.com

Reprinted with permission of Dr. Mache Seibel ©2011. All rights reserved.

by providing consistent additional value. Chad recently spoke to a prospect who shared with him that over the past year she has been successful in building her distribution list. She has indicated that she added 10,000 people to her database, which represents great marketing success.

Yet, when Chad asked her how she nurtures the database with consistent value she said: "Oh, I haven't done anything with it yet!" And you may wonder where we get our material? You can't make this stuff up!

One of the key mistakes we see is that people are still driving the results of the search efforts to their homepage instead of the appropriate landing page. This is a tremendous misuse of potential conversion.

If you wish to learn more about search engine marketing and optimization, here are some excellent resources:

· www.searchenginenews.com
· www.bruceclay.com
· www.seomoz.org
· www.seomoz.org/beginners-guide-to-seo
· www.searchengineland.com
· www.wilsonweb.com
· www.searchengineguide.com
· www.searchenginewatch.com
· www.seobook.com
· www.wordtracker.com
· www.webposition.com
· www.google.com/webmasters
· www.mashable.com
· www.mattcutts.com/blog
· www.youtube.com/user/GoogleWebmasterHelp

There are many tools available to provide you with analytics about your site. We know the expert mathematicians and statisticians are going to be all over us for this but we believe that these tools are a good reference point to review every once in a while (quarterly or semi-annually), and you should not overly obsess about them. One such tool is Google Analytics, which provides good information and is rather easy to implement, and can easily be run for any period of time range.

Figure 9.5 shows a graph representing the number of visits per day, which may be helpful to track your particular marketing initiatives.

Figure 9.6 is a screenshot showing access to the site ranked by the most popular mobile devices and shows the number of visits, average

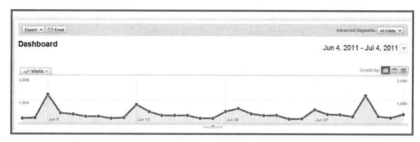

Figure 9.5: **Visits per day**

time on the site, and bounce rate (visitors who exited the site from the first landing page they arrived at). This should help identify which mobile devices your site should be tested on as well as, possibly, the consideration of creating special apps.

Figure 9.7 on page 206 is similar to the previous one and ranks access to the site by country. This should help the determination whether your site should be translated to other popular languages.

Figure 9.8 on page 206 shows a Google Analytics result ranking the access to the site by browsers. This should help identify which browsers should be tested.

Figure 9.9 on page 207 shows how visitors arrive at your site by typing your address or using their bookmarks, from search engines, or

These mobile devices sent 1,074 visits via 6 operating systems

	Operating System	None	Visits ↓	Pages/Visit	Avg. Time on Site	% New Visits	Bounce Rate
1.	iPad		453	3.03	00:03:18	52.98%	51.43%
2.	iPhone		440	1.61	00:01:33	49.77%	75.23%
3.	Android		137	2.00	00:02:02	59.12%	67.88%
4.	BlackBerry		30	1.23	00:00:17	50.00%	83.33%
5.	iPod		8	1.25	00:00:33	75.00%	75.00%
6.	SymbianOS		6	1.50	00:01:17	100.00%	66.67%

Visits: 1,074, Site Avg: 8.61%. Pages/Visit: 2.24, Site Avg: 2.59 (-13.29%). Avg. Time on Site: 00:02:18, Site Avg: 00:02:55 (-21.37%). % New Visits: 52.79%, Site Avg: 42.80% (23.34%). Bounce Rate: 64.43%, Site Avg: 57.24% (12.57%)

Figure 9.6: **Mobile device access**

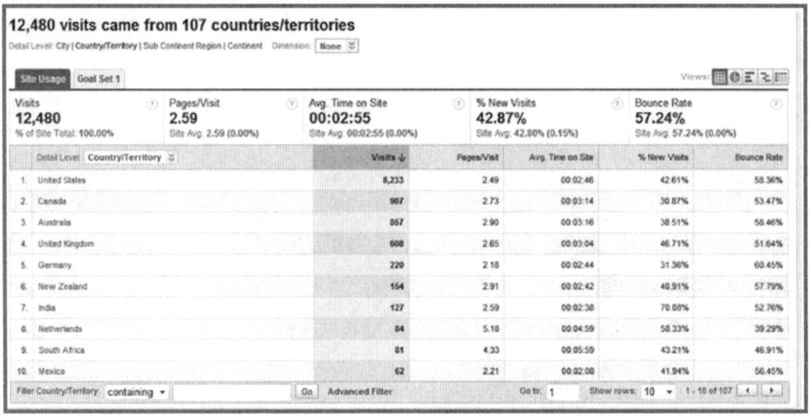

Figure 9.7: **Access by country**

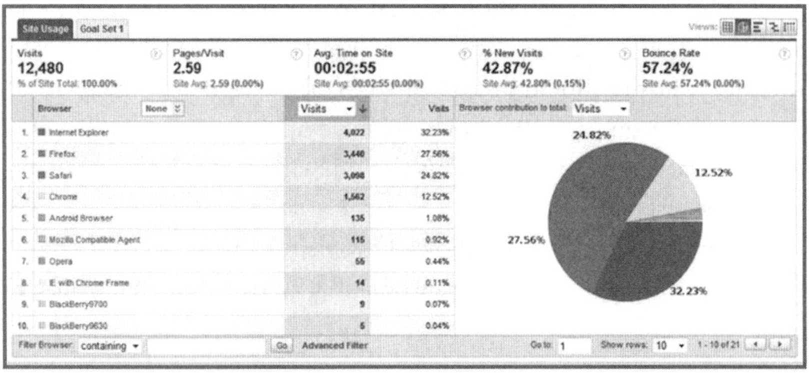

Figure 9.8: **Access by browser**

other sites that link to yours. This should help identify which browsers should be tested.

These represent just a small sample of an impressive array of analytics that can be viewed to determine many useful marketing factors, as well as analytics about pages and their access. (Complete books have been dedicated to this one topic and it is beyond the scope of our book.)

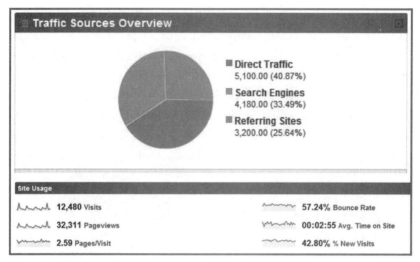

Figure 9.9: **Traffic sources**

Are video landing pages more effective than text landing pages? When questions like these are asked and are worth exploring, the A/B testing method has been quite popular to help us decide. This method requires that you create a couple of pages; for example, one landing page with the embedded video and one with just the text. You then segment your client database into two and send one group the link to the first page and the second group the link to the second page. The actual results combined with Google Analytics should then provide the answer to which page is more successful. You can easily run this test yourself.

If you have committed to implement search engine marketing as part of your strategy, you need to recognize the importance of time and adjustments to track your results. *We recommend a minimum of 9 to 12 months to do so.* You should have a starting snapshot of your analytics before any such campaign is launched so you are able to measure your progress.

As long as the human race has existed, we have been "in search of . . . ." Search engine marketing seems to be the digital 21st century extension of this phenomenon. We all have our documented successes and that of our clients and we are not here to argue with others' success. So, should you invest your time, energy, and dollars into search engine marketing?

It depends. If your target audience consists primarily of corporate buyers, driven to your high-end services, the likelihood of these buyers searching for you online in order to hire you is quite remote. Yet, if your target audience consists of consumers looking for products such as books, booklets, CDs, workshops, webinars, teleseminars (and even mentoring, coaching, training, and speaking services), you may want to leverage search engine marketing as part of your strategy.

It is your call. We intended here to make it an informed one.

Why Social Media
Is an Oxymoron
(or maybe just a moron)

Social media and all that online jazz

Imagine you just awoke from a Rip VanWinkle nap (say, 100 years), finding yourself in the bustling center of New York's Times Square, where you are given the ability to eavesdrop on any conversation you wish, where you can quickly check out individual profiles, or even listen to their previous conversations, where it is customary to also engage in conversations with strangers who are conducting short and random conversations with other strangers, while many are trying to sell you and others their products and services.

You are also told that this is the hottest new place where you must conduct your future business or you will forever be left behind or put back into another long nap (which, after this experience, may actually be a more comforting choice). You then quickly discover that just about everyone roaming the streets is a so-called expert, making it challenging to distinguish between genuine talent and charlatans. Even the hobos, who are loudly cursing and roaming the streets, declare they own the desired secret decoder ring. Welcome to social media![1]

Let's first discuss our definition of social media: "The use of various technologies to create mutual connections with personal and professional contacts." This includes the exploration of mutual interests; sharing of ideas, experiences, wisdom, and expertise; gaining credibility; nurturing relationships; having fun; providing and soliciting answers to questions; and conducting business.

Let us also suggest that social media is an oxymoron because it is so often anti-social—profane, argumentative, loud, ill-informed, full of scams, and so on. (Like a bad Boston bar at closing, where everyone is drunk and nasty, as we heard one wag comment.) It is also probably the perfect addiction tool for a person suffering from an attention deficit disorder.

Where else can you get distracted with thousands of messages instantaneously flashing before your eyes and fighting for your momentary attention? Our intent is to offer clarification and pragmatic ideas so you, too, can leverage social media for success in your business while remaining sane and less addicted. Yet, and as you would expect from us by now, unless we can substantiate a pragmatic use, we are going to employ a contrarian approach about this topic. So before you fully commit and possibly get frustrated about wasting all your remaining waking moments exploring and figuring out this new maze, read on.

When it comes to technology platforms available to facilitate social interactions, the options are vast, which is actually one of the key and most frustrating challenges many of our clients face. In recent years, we've seen the proliferation and creation of new technology platforms and the claims that theirs are about to change the future of computing

---

[1] As we write this, the phone hacking scandal with Rupert Murdoch's empire in the United Kingdom is still developing, including police payoffs, and hacking into the phone of those who were victims and even those who died.

and human interactions. Here is a quick look at a few of the innovation dinosaurs left behind—soon to be.

When it came to email and online interactions, America On Line (AOL) used to rule the world. (We like to call this Amateurs on Line.) Google Wave was supposed to become the future of email and collaboration. MySpace used to be the best and largest platform for social interaction and is now completely overshadowed by Facebook. As of the writing of this book, Google Plus is creating a strong buzz and is claiming to soon replace Facebook and Twitter and become the new king in town. So unless the focus of your business is technology, internet, or social media, and you have no better use of your time and resources, we suggest you let other experts, such as us, figure out and showcase the practical use of leveraging technologies and not jump on the latest fad.

Therefore, we will focus primarily on effective social media concepts and the most popular business platforms you should consider using, such as Facebook, Twitter, and LinkedIn. We will also touch on other social media platforms such as blogs, YouTube, iTunes, forums (online communities), and a few others.

Have you ever wondered how many people access these social media platforms? The growth numbers are staggering and are increasing daily. Because of this buzz, popularity, the gold-rush-like promises, and the "me too" syndrome, hundreds of millions of people are rushing to create their profiles on these platforms. There are over 100 million LinkedIn users, over 175 million Twitter users, and Facebook claims to have over 750 million active users, where 70 percent are outside the United States, 50 percent log on each day, the average user has 130 friends, and a third of the users access it through their mobile devices. (These will be higher by the time you read this.)

A *Harvard Business Review* study[2] showed that 10 percent of Twitter users generate 90 percent of the activity, which suggests a smaller

---

[2] http://blogs.hrb.org/cs/2009/06/new_twitter_esearch_men_follo.html

than anticipated users' involvement, of which most are broadcasting messages rather than engaging in genuine social conversations.

So are your buyers socializing or interacting on the various social media platforms? It depends. If your target buyers are consumers, entrepreneurs, and service providers, it is very probable that they are there. If your target buyers are corporate clients, it is quite unlikely that these buyers are there. Of course, there are some rare exceptions to this, *but corporate buyers are not surfing the social media platforms to look for service providers.*[3]

Virtual Reality

Do not confuse the recreational and entertainment aspects of the social media platforms with legitimate professional marketing requirements. You can't "amuse yourself into marketing."

However, keep in mind that most technology companies have strong presence on these platforms and they participate often and try to lead the way. Also, most corporations have a strong social media presence as they realize that their consumers are there and they want to increase the positive interaction and influence on them. Just go to Facebook, for example, and search for some of the larger global organizations and their brands such as Starbucks, BMW, Mont Blanc, and others. They are there as are millions of their followers.

Finally, let us also share with you these two secrets:

- The people most vociferous about social media are clearly those who stand to gain by it, giving seminars, providing coaching, and somehow making money by encouraging use. It's almost like a huge Ponzi scheme in some respects. We're reminded of

---

[3] They primarily use peer referrals and high-profile experts with intellectual property highly visible.

Y2K, or the guy with the pinky ring and Cadillac who rents the hotel room for a presentation to get you to buy soapsuds and "recruit new members" in a multilevel marketing scheme.

· If your target buyers are experts or so-called experts in areas of technology, search engine optimization, social media, internet strategies, life happiness, inspiration, and such, guess what? You struck gold! But watch for them swarming at you and probably us after they read this book.

Why social media, then? People have been overwhelmed with ordinary and tiresome marketing messages through various delivery channels as the new trends have seen their growing trust in their peers, friends, and colleagues to influence, recommend, and validate their purchases. Assuming your target buyers are spending some of their time on these platforms, here are some of the reasons why you should then consider getting involved with social media:

· It helps you increase the possibility of creating a community around your brand while developing and nurturing trusting relationships.

· Using social media can leverage the exponential power of your connections so a friend of a friend may just discover you that way.

· You never know where the next hit comes from. Your next customer may just have found you on one of the social media platforms.

· Social media complements the visitor's access preference. Some may like to contact you via email, some by phone, some via Twitter, and some through Facebook.

· It increases the likelihood of the viral effect. If someone likes your content, they are likely to immediately share it with many in their community who may share with many in theirs. This creates the possibility of exponential viral phenomena.

· Using social media demonstrates your embracing of technology to better connect with your audience.

- It helps improve the traffic to your site and the conversion rate from stranger to a prospect to a client.
- Replace interruption-based marketing with marketing gravity.
- Reach out to people who are already communicating there.
- Track discussions and comments about you, your brands, competitors, and partners.
- You can track what other credible individuals are saying.
- Quickly participate in discussions where you may ask or answer questions.
- Using social media allows you to amplify your voice and especially the voice of your clients.

Traps and myths

Trap: Wasting too much time. This is by far the biggest trap we see our clients fall into. Our recommendation is 30 minutes per day or less.

Myth: You must follow and friend everyone that follows or friends you. We recommend you only follow credible individuals (check out their posts, profiles, and websites for credibility).

Trap: Driving through like a bull in a china shop. Spend some time checking out the landscape, whose posts you like, the caliber of their contribution, and their frequency. Then start participating.

Myth: The social media platforms will help create and build your brand. You must create and nurture your brand first and then expect these platforms to help nurture it further, and not the other way around.

Trap: Social media has replaced traditional marketing. Don't fall for it or let these "experts" influence you. People still flock to hear a great speaker, attend important conferences, and purchase their hard-copy books.

In order to increase the appearance of your content on these multiple platforms and reduce your labor intensity, we recommend you interface your blog, Facebook, LinkedIn, and Twitter accounts. Your blog entries will automatically use their title to create a tweet, which will then be posted both in terms of the status as well as the entire post into LinkedIn and Facebook. We realize that this is somewhat redundant, yet some may be active on one platform and not another, so this does make sense.

The social media platforms can play a role for you, as we've indicated, but it's important to judge ROI. Don't confuse whatever recreational allure they hold for you with legitimate business purposes, and never abandon marketing gravity approaches to spend more time on social media.

Having created our caveats, here are some specifics.

Facebook

Let us now unveil the mystery of Facebook, what you need to know to become effective and use it as a productive tool for your business. Also, for the remainder of the chapter, and in order to save on our digital ink, we will use the abbreviation FB to represent Facebook. We assume in this section that you are using FB as a business tool and not for personal reasons only.

When it comes to FB, the four most important concepts you need to master are: Profile page, Business pages, Groups, and Events. Your profile page is used to establish your profile. You should set up only one profile page for yourself. Business pages are also called "fan pages," "like pages," or "pages." You may set up a business page to showcase your company or you may even set up multiple business pages to showcase your various brands. Groups are used to create communities around your brand or interests. Events are used to promote physical and virtual events. Let us get into a bit more detail on each.

Profile pages

These allow you to establish your identity on FB and make connections with other contacts that FB calls "friends." It all starts with your profile page, which is required before you can do anything else on FB. This page allows you to add your personal information, photos, and videos, include your blog postings, connect with your friends, and post on the page called your "wall."

Your profile should reflect your accomplishments, interests, important links, and client results. See the profile example in Figure 10.1 of one of our colleagues and partners, Patricia Fripp.

A key issue many struggle with is whether to set up a profile page for personal or business use, or actually for both. Since the purpose of

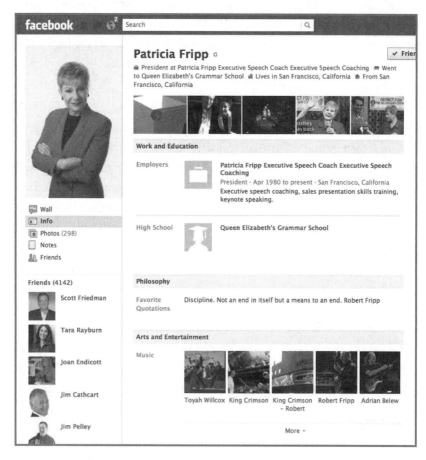

Figure 10.1: **A profile page**
Reprinted with permission of Patricia Fripp ©2011. All rights reserved.

the business page is all about your business presence on FB, you have a couple of options to consider:

- Set up your profile page for personal and business use and accept such connections, yet recognize that the essence of this is for business and very little or no personal interaction. *The challenge at times is when your personal connections may be posting ideas that may be irrelevant or even damaging for your business contacts to view.* Although you can always remove the connection (un-friend) or hide their posts from others, this could be an issue that influences FB's effectiveness for you.

Virtual Reality

If you intend to use Facebook for business reasons, then don't make it a personal entertainment center or recreational destination for you or others.

- Set up your profile page for personal use only and limit your contacts to only allow connections with friends and family. When doing so, we suggest you limit considerably what the public can view by *fine-tuning your privacy settings* (see Figure 10.2 on page 218). We also suggest you modify your personal photo to incorporate a short sentence (at the bottom of the photo) indicating this is your personal page and you conduct business on your business page with the link to that page. Include that link in the "Basic Information" section of your profile as well. Then set up a business page for your business or brands promotion use only. The slight challenge we see today with the creation of business pages is that FB requires your future contacts to click on the "like" button in order to connect with you, and some don't bother to do this.
- Combine both options above, which means that you end up setting your profile page for personal and business use as well as

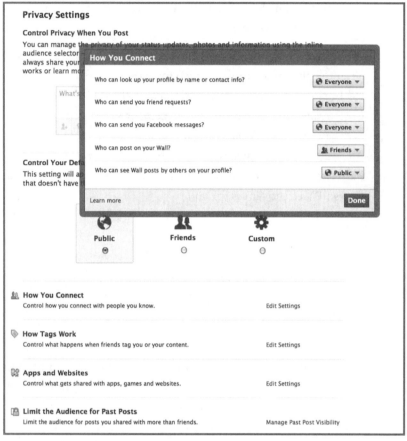

Figure 10.2: **Fine-tuning your privacy settings**

set up a business page. This is our preferred way of setting this up, although all these options make sense and are dependent on your personal and business needs and preferences.

Keep in mind that as of right now FB only allows up to 5,000 connections through your personal profile page.

Business pages

These allow you much more flexibility in setting up the various pages to describe your business and your various brands. The good news about these pages is that you may set up multiple business pages, with the flexibility of setting up multiple tabs per page, and there is no limit to the number of connections you may create.

In order to view the business pages that you have connected (by pressing the "Link" button), go to your personal profile page, click on "Info," and then you will see them listed in the "Activities and Interests" section. Notice in the example in Figure 10.3 how our colleague, Randy

Figure 10.3: **Effective business page for an individual**
Reprinted with permission of Randy Gage ©2011. All rights reserved.

Figure 10.4: **Effective business page for a company**
Reprinted with permission of Audimute Soundproofing ©2011. All rights reserved.

Gage, has set up his business page with the various tabs (top left) and options of: Wall, Info, Friend Activity, YouTube, Events, Products, News, Photos, Welcome, Twitter, Discussions, LinkedIn, and My info. And also notice in Figure 10.4, how Audimute has created their effective business page for their products and brand.

Groups

FB groups are your way of creating your own community or joining an already established one. They allow you to share ideas with like-minded people. We have written an entire chapter on the power, importance, and necessity of creating communities around your brand. We are also proud to have created and nurtured www.AlansForums.com, one of the best and most active online communities in the world for professional consultants, coaches, and related service providers. We find the Groups concept on FB to be an easy and free way of establishing such communities.

However, it is extremely limited in functionality, robustness, the user's experience, and reflecting and establishing your own brand. So, if you are attempting to simply experiment with creating such a community with no serious plans for dramatic immediate success, then this is a good starting point. If, on the other hand, you wish to build a strong community around your brand quickly, *do not use FB to do so*. Either read Chapter 3 dedicated to this, or contact us. We do suggest you join several existing groups, observe them, and then participate by interacting and contributing your wisdom. This will provide a free "hands-on" experience.

Events

FB events are a great way to promote your physical events such as: public workshops, seminars, speaking, and training engagements. It is also an outstanding way of promoting your virtual events such as webinars, teleseminars, and online events streaming.

The great thing about this is that you can create a FB event in seconds and then promote it to all your connections in a few more seconds. You then can track who is attending or not, have others see who is attending (which could influence others), and also enable people to promote the events to their connections, which creates an exponential marketing effort if done well.

Figure 10.5 and 10.6 are two screenshots depicting an example wherein one of our clients, Kelli Richards, promoting her interview event, invited Chad to attend, who then confirmed his attendance and also promoted the event to his connections.

Years ago, when Chad first started to use FB, he asked this question on his FB wall status: "Is anyone seriously reading or even paying attention to these silly status messages?" A few minutes later, his nephew from Australia replied: "That is what we live for!" Although probably a humorous but sad commentary of what may epitomize the trivial interest level of FB members, it also made us wonder: Could it be that some are looking for quick, stimulating, interesting, and provocative ideas to interact with or reflect upon, or is it possible that they have nothing better to do? Let us share with you some conceptual differences between such posts and ours. Here is a random and quick sample of some of the posts on our walls today, and please keep in mind that these are from global entrepreneurs and service providers:

Figure 10.5: **An event page**
Reprinted with permission of Kelli Richards ©2011. All rights reserved.

Figure 10.6: **Event promoted via viral marketing**

Thinking of taking surfing lessons later this week. Been watching them and I think I can do it!

Eating healthy, went for a brisk walk.

Missed my flight this morning for the first time in about 9 years.

Oooommm . . . "I love my life." "I love my life." "I LOVE MY LIFE!" Repeat this all day long to yourself & out loud to others. Wishing you a peace-fully & delightfully glorious Tuesday.

Do something amazing today!

This quote hit me between the eyes so I have to share it . . . "He that would live in peace and at ease, must not speak all he knows, nor judge all he sees." —Benjamin Franklin

View from my coaching room—just counted 19 bunnies!

Marketing contest is underway. The votes are fascinating. I love seeing the numbers and what people think. Check out my blog or search on FB.

Not exactly chatter you want your business affairs submerged in. On the other hand, here is a quick sample of some of Chad's and Alan's posts:

Language controls discussions, discussions control relationships, relationships control business. Watch your language. (Figure 10.7 shows how this thought has started to generate a discussion.)

Confront, don't enable, poor behavior: "You've cancelled 3 meetings at the last minute. I can't work with you if you do that."

Effective Podcasting. Ever wonder? Listen now: http://bit.ly/qq5eKt

In the first 2 minutes of your speech, the audience determines to what extent they'll listen to the rest.

Changing Your Small Talk to Big Talk http://bit.ly/n5VG3H

Requisites for newcomer to consulting: High self-esteem, six months of expenses in bank.

How to Handle Objections: http://t.co/qFtm3XZ

Requisites for veterans in consulting: Building brand, becoming IP, thinking big.

Viral marketing incorporates exponential power by leveraging the web, people, and your outstanding content.

How easy is it to contact you? Just had to call a colleague but no phone # on his site or email signature!

Alan Weiss

Language controls discussions, discussions control relationships, relationships control business. Watch your language.

Like · Comment · @BentleyGTCSpeed on Twitt · July 17 at 3:45pm via Twitter · ✺

Anastasia L. Turchetta and 7 others like this.

Luca Marcolin Thoughts control Language... Watch your thoughts.
July 17 at 4:15pm · Like · 👍 3

Alan Weiss Really? Can you think without words?
July 17 at 4:44pm · Like

Luca Marcolin Dear Alan, you see, in my broken English, language was the words spoken, not the thoughts; I absolutely agree with you, we cannot think without words. Let's rephrase it, before you speak, think!
July 17 at 4:51pm · Like

Alan Weiss Why don't we just go with my original?
July 17 at 8:33pm · Like

Luca Marcolin Sure Alan! I just wanted to rephrase my comment to better confirm and support you post.
July 18 at 1:53am · Like · 👍 1

John Wesey Hello Alan, in as much as i don't have any problem with your post, i still agree with Luca. Thought/thinking is the warehouse where the language, using words are packaged and organised before it is uttered. If the warehouse is not organised, the businesses will not exist.
July 18 at 7:10am · Like

Alan Weiss I'm trying to make a pragmatic point for people engaged in sales and you're dealing with an esoteric, philosophical point. You want people to organize their mental warehouse? Then you write that book. I write books about how to pragmatically prepare and close business.
July 18 at 4:31pm · Like · 👍 2

Figure 10.7: **Valuable posts lead to discussions**

How frequently do you have something new to say? Increase your success by saying something unique and often. Consider how unique, qualitative, and provocative your posts are. Notice in the preceeding list our incorporation of effective hyperlinks to the proper landing pages on our sites. And finally, if you are attempting to strengthen your thought leader position, why not demonstrate original thoughts and quote yourself—not others?

So what *should* you post on FB?

- Since we have previously recommended that you interface your FB account with other social media platforms such as your blog, Twitter, and LinkedIn accounts, by virtue of posting on these platforms, your FB will automatically get populated with content from these platforms.
- You may post directly on your wall and populate it with interesting topics about your business, your life (in serious and limited moderation), as well as stories about your clients' successes and best practices.
- Incorporate text, photos which most seem to enjoy, videos that are uploaded directly to FB or are shared from YouTube, and links to landing pages.
- Invitation to physical and virtual events such as public workshops, webinars, and teleseminars.
- Interesting ideas worth mentioning with links to landing pages on your site and blog to intrigue them to click on these links and land on your sites. Once they enter your site, use the "stickiness" approach by offering value to capture their contact information so you may then convert them into a prospect or a client.
- Valuable references to others that are of great interest for your clients.

How often should you post to FB? We recommend at least three times per week and no more than three times per day. Others may recommend that you post as often and frequently as possible, especially to "capture" as many readers as possible throughout the day and night. But we say, don't! You are not a news aggregator or want to be perceived as a spammer. So one final drum roll, please, as you are going to hear us say this for the umpteenth time: valuable, unique, consistent, and provocative content. There you go. As simple yet as complex as that!

Although this seems to be obvious for most of us, here's what not to post. So here you go. Anything pertaining to: the frequency or habits of your bodily functions, food intake, and exercise schedule; etiquette (or lack of) habits; schedule of trivial events such as when you arrived at the office; silly jokes or references to activities that diminish your credibility and intellectual firepower.

The key is to remember that you're using this for business and not personal reasons.

Friending

The concept of creating connections with people on FB is called "friending." This means that you may want to initiate the request to friend and connect with someone else. Or, you may receive a request from someone who wants to connect with you. Or, you may receive a connection recommendation from someone who wants to "introduce" you virtually to someone else.

Should you friend people, and who should you friend? We recommend you friend people who represent your potential buyers and recommenders, or ones that may stimulate your mind. Since our target audience comprises consultants, entrepreneurs, speakers, authors, coaches, and boutique firm owners, as long as they fall into one of these categories and they seem to be established, we friend them. This is one of the places where our buyers hang out, so we are there.

An example: When logging on to FB, Chad noticed a person who was actually recommended for him to friend by FB. He clicked on her profile and quickly learned from her profile page that she is a speaker, author, and also conducts workshops. She has an established website with 3,000 friends on FB and seems to be active on her wall with interesting things to say. *Definitely a potential friend,* he said to himself. When clicking on the "Add Friend" button, Chad then overrode the FB category to a "prospect" that enables him to better target his lists during events promotions.

Chad checks out the validity of profiles, business focus, and whether they are established or not when others request to friend him.

Figure 10.8: **Friending**

This entire process takes only a few seconds and is repeated several times a week so our connection database grows.

When most struggle at increasing their database of potential buyer connection, we find this method to be one of the easiest ways to grow and nurture your databases and start creating relationships.

Vital considerations

· The content on your business pages and events pages gets indexed by search engines such as Google, which is a good thing. Your profile page information does not get indexed, which is also a good thing.

· Create a friendly FB URL so you may promote it easily. For example, here are our Facebook URLs where you are welcome to send us your friend request. Heck, you are reading our book, which is a brilliant move in our book:

– www.facebook.com/ChadBarrGroup

- www.facebook.com/RockStarOfConsulting

Keep in mind that you may want to consider purchasing your own domain, which can then get redirected to your Facebook profile or business page. So, for example, www.ChadBarrFace book.com is then redirected to www.facebook.com/ChadBarr Group

· We strongly recommend you consider your privacy issues when posting on FB. The potential vulnerability is great, as nothing is truly private when it comes to your online posts. So before you press that "Return" button, just ask yourself if what you are about to post—whether it is text, photos, audios, or videos—has the potential of damaging your brand. If there is even a slight chance of this, use the delete button instead.

· Review the business pages below for effective and powerful use of Facebook to strengthen the brand and open dialogue with customers:

- www.facebook.com/wholefoods
- www.facebook.com/Levenger
- www.facebook.com/McDonalds
- www.facebook.com/Southwest
- www.facebook.com/Starbucks
- www.facebook.com/timferriss
- www.facebook.com/JeffreyGitomer

· Create a FB badge that can then be easily imported to and displayed on your website and blog. This way, when visitors arrive at your site or blog, they can click on your FB badge and be taken to your FB profile or business page and connect with you.

· FB is quickly and dramatically evolving its advertising engine, which allows you to target ads that will display for your potential buyers. The potential here is tremendous, as you are now able to fine-tune the target audience and the messages you are promoting.

· There is a potential danger zone when it comes to FB. If you are flagged as engaging in questionable tactics that may break the rules, you then run the risk of your profile being cancelled, which will cause you to lose all your content and connections.

CASE STUDY
How Genuine Inquiries and Conversations May Lead to Business

Here is a quick story from Chad to conclude this section. "A while ago I noticed some familiar photos on someone's FB profile. They were shot in Israel, where I was born, with additional photos taken by this person while delivering his speech at the University of Tel Aviv. Intrigued, I commented on several of his photos as to how beautiful they are and the fact that they brought back such great childhood memories. I also sent him an email and asked if he'd be willing to share with me how he got the speaking engagement. He replied immediately, telling me that he just landed on his returned flight home and would be delighted to share some more. We connected a couple of days later and after our discussion and probably checking me out online, he made a personal introduction on my behalf to the people who could hire me in Tel Aviv."

So as you can see, there is a lot you can do. You just need to be creative, pay attention to opportunities, and seize the moment.

Facebook is a legitimate phenomenon. But that doesn't make it all things to all people, especially for marketing purposes. Be discerning, and if Facebook is going to be in your professional plans, then invest the small highly focused amount of time we suggested earlier in this section.

Twitter

We both predicted that Twitter was going to be a passing fad. Even Walt Mossberg, the technology columnist for *The Wall Street Journal*, when asked during his presentation at one of our events, had a similar answer. Luckily, we have not bet our future on the survival of Twitter or any such technologies. Although we resisted it at first, since it provided us and our clients with little or no pragmatic value, we have to admit that we have grown to like it and have fun with it.

From our perspective, Twitter is the ultimate manifestation of the ability to provide quick, pithy, and succinct value in short sentences of 140 characters or less (much less if you want to be "retweeted"). Even our online discussions with our contacts (called followers) contain the same characters restrictions, which works great for our business model.

So what is Twitter? It is a micro-blogging platform that enables you to communicate with others in 140 characters or less. This communication may be between one and many (@Reply) in public format, which means when a person posts, anyone can view. It may be between one and another (@Reply) in public format, which also means that a note that is sent from one person to another may be viewed by anyone. And the final format (DM) is one-to-one in private, which means that only the recipient may view this direct message.

Why should you consider using Twitter?

- Create your online accountability partner, which will "force" you to post or tweet and increase the scope of your body of work. Many of our clients have followed our advice to compile their tweets into an ebook or booklet such as *The Cool Guide to Social Media Success*, or *32 Strategy Deadly Mistakes to Avoid*.
- Help strengthen your online brand creation and create and nurture your online voice.
- Easy way to share your value and intellectual property.
- Communicate with clients, journalists, colleagues, and partners, and use the tool to engage them.
- Easily search (www.Search.Twitter.com) what others are tweeting, which will give you ideas on what is being said about you, your company and brands, as well as competitive information.

- Promote physical and virtual events, products, and services provided by you or others.
- Drive traffic to your site's landing pages.
- Use as a customer service tool, especially to communicate urgent messages if and when necessary. Also ask what can you do to better help them.
- Easy way to increase your contact database.
- Connect with journalists, thought leaders, and popular bloggers to learn, share, and make connections.
- Contact advertisers and ask them to place ads with you, especially when your brand and number of contacts grow.
- Receive "live" questions during physical and virtual events. You can monitor the twitter hashtag tweets and then select the ones desired.
- Have people submit their questions for physical and virtual events and have a moderator monitor that channel and relay the question to the person conducting the event. TV stations do this quite often now.
- Ask your followers questions and usually get quick answers, which can then be virally spread to their followers.
- Register complaints that have popular support. Everyone from airlines to consumer products monitor Twitter and seek to ameliorate complaints by trying to please the offended party.[4]
- It's fun.

To get started, you first need to create your personal or company profile, or both. If your organization employs multiple people and you are going to have several of them use Twitter as the consolidated voice of the organization, we would then recommend you set up a company profile for all to use and contribute to. Otherwise, only set up your personal profile on Twitter for you to use. In certain situations, it may

---

[4] We heartily recommend an app for this as well: Gripe.

make sense to set up your personal profile in conjunction with the organization profile.

When setting up your profile, select a friendly name (no spaces), which will become your Twitter URL that clearly identifies you, your organization, or your brand. Indicate your value proposition, link to your site's landing page, your photo, and a professional-looking background (and not the Twitter default). When selecting a profile name, Twitter always adds the @ sign as the prefix of the name. Since both our Twitter names were already taken, when setting up our personal accounts, Chad selected @ChadBarrGroup, and the actual referenced URL given by Twitter is http://twitter.com/ChadBarrGroup. Alan has selected @BentleyGTCSpeed, with the URL of http://twitter.com/BentleyGTCSpeed. (See Figures 10.9 and 10.10.)

Figure 10.9: **Chad's Twitter homepage**

Figure 10.10: **Alan's Twitter homepage**

(We welcome you to follow us on Twitter and receive our updates and remarkable content.)

A couple of important side notes: You may want to purchase and create your own domain name that points to Twitter, as in this example: www.ChadBarr.com/Twitter.

You may want to consider linking your Twitter profile to a special landing page on your website that is dedicated for visitors from Twitter. You can then welcome them and provide them with a special offer on that page.

Who should you follow? It depends. If your brand is as strong, provocative, and contrarian as Alan's, you then follow no one. It is sure to provoke many who then come out furious and start questioning every aspect of your online existence. They also argue as to why you are not following the imaginary "Twitter etiquette book," which interestingly enough was probably created by them!

However, most decide to reciprocate by following each other. We suggest you then follow individuals who are in your target audience—clients, prospective clients, journalists, thought leaders, interesting bloggers, colleagues, competitors, and others like them. The benefit is that you can then easily and quickly "listen" to the ones you want to pay attention to. Once such tool to aggregate all tweets, which we will discuss shortly, is TweetDeck.

Virtual Reality

Twitter provides great discipline in forcing you to produce pithy, high-value content within severe limitations, IF you use it for branding and viral marketing.

Search for individuals you want to follow, and once you find them, simply click on the "Follow" button. You then may wish to search for the people they are following or that are following them in order to get ideas for others you may want to include. Once you start following people, others will want to follow you. When that happens, and depending on your setup, you may get an email notification or simply log on to Twitter and when clicking on your profile you may click on "Following" to see the ones that follow you. We recommend you connect and reciprocate with those who are credible, which can usually be determined in a few seconds of clicking and reading.

To attract others to follow you, make sure you incorporate your Twitter URL link everywhere possible, such as: your website, blog, email signature, business cards, newsletters, and articles. See Figure 10.11 on page 236 for example of embedding the Twitter URL in its widget among the other social media widgets.

You are now ready to start tweeting, which is quite simple to do. If you are using the Twitter application vs. others such as TweetDeck, enter your post or tweet in the "What's Happening" box. You may enter the following:

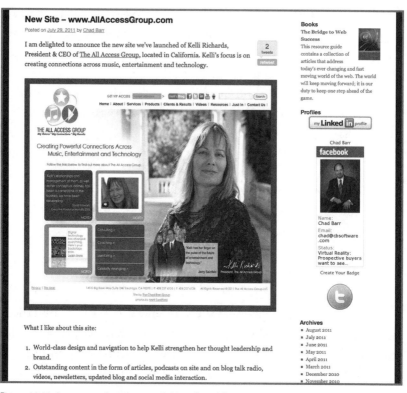

New Site – www.AllAccessGroup.com

Posted on July 29, 2011 by Chad Barr

I am delighted to announce the new site we've launched of Kelli Richards, President & CEO of The All Access Group, located in California. Kelli's focus is on creating connections across music, entertainment and technology.

Books
The Bridge to Web Success
This resource guide contains a collection of articles that address today's ever changing and fast moving world of the web. The world will keep moving forward; it is our duty to keep one step ahead of the game.

Profiles

Archives
- August 2011
- July 2011
- June 2011
- May 2011
- April 2011
- March 2011
- December 2010
- November 2010

What I like about this site:

1. World-class design and navigation to help Kelli strengthen her thought leadership and brand.
2. Outstanding content in the form of articles, podcasts on site and on blog talk radio, videos, newsletters, updated blog and social media interaction.

Figure 10.11: Incorporating your social media widget
Reprinted with permission of Kelli Richards ©2011. All rights reserved.

- The text of the message you wish to tweet.
- A message to someone that anyone may view, by using the @ Reply concept, which represents the person's Twitter screen name. So for example, I may want to send this message to Alan: "Completing Chapter 10 of my book with @BentleyGTCSpeed scheduled for publication this year." This message will be then displayed and viewable by all who are following me or Alan.
- A private message (DM), only viewable by the recipient. Here is an example: "DM @BentleyGTCSpeed looking forward to a great dinner & wine this evening," but keep in mind that *you can send a direct message only to people who follow you.*

- Someone else's tweet that you want to share with your followers, which is called a "retweet" (RT). Here is an example: "RT @ BentleyGTCSpeed: Success, not perfection. Focus on the project, not everything you think needs improving." This method actually allows me to repurpose someone else's tweets, in this case, Alan's.

- A hashtag, or the # sign is a way to categorize a tweet for easier search or create a special reference to a workshop or an event. For example, if we wanted to categorize our tweet under marketing, the post may look like this: "The concept of #marketing gravity is essential when reviewing the products one wants to add to their business." Notice the use of the # sign before marketing, which is then easily searchable. Another common use for the hashtag is to share it with the participants of an event so they may tweet it to their followers. It is a great way to promote your event before, during, and after. For example, if we wanted to use this concept to promote our "Product Experience" workshop for 2012, we would then tweet before the event and ask participants to tweet during the event and use the code #ProdExp2012," which allows the same search and retrieval as mentioned above.

- When referencing a URL, it needs to be shortened so it fits within the 140 characters restriction. There are many such services, yet the one we usually use is www.bit.ly, which requires you to first set up an account with them. You then can shorten any URL and reference it in your tweet. It's a free service. We also recommend bitly.com for these purposes, which is also free.[5]

An idea you may want to consider is to search on Twitter for topics of interest. Once you find these tweets, *start interacting and engaging the person by direct messages (DM) or @Reply*. DO NOT spam them, but offer value and suggest you help them.

---

[5] For example, www.contrarianconsulting.com would be reduced by bitly.com to http://bit.ly/OoMlg, which makes it much easier to use in a tweet.

One of our favorite tools to use on our desktop as well as iPad and iPhone is the TweetDeck application. It allows you to easily organize and aggregate others' tweets similarly to the way Google Reader does for RSS feeds for blogs and such. This enables Chad to quickly track his clients' tweets in one column with other interesting thought leaders in another. See Figure 10.12.

Additional Twitter online resources:

http://hootsuite.com/
http://twitterfeed.com/
http://twellow.com/
http://wefollow.com/
http://ping.fm/
http://cotweet.com/
www.socialoomph.com/
http://twitpic.com
www.hashtag.org/
http://whatthetrend.com/

Figure 10.12: **Using TweetDeck**

What should you tweet about?

- Tips, how-to, and your featured intellectual property.
- Short, provocative statements with links to take the visitor to your targeted landing pages.
- Interesting things you are doing that are of value to your audience.
- Promotion of events.
- News worthy of sharing.
- Suggest they tweet your tweet and share with others; remember, if you don't ask, the answer is always no.
- Interesting information to entice readers to click which will take them to the landing page.
- Your retweets of others or promoting others' products and services or intellectual property.
- Contact someone public @Reply or privately DM.

As we have indicated previously, when it comes to privacy, do not take the internet for granted. Anything can surface one day. So do not write things that you may regret later on. When it comes to the internet, *The Good, the Bad, and the Ugly* is a great movie analogy.

Finally, if you want to assess your clout on Twitter, we love Klout. com, which is compatible with Twitter and Facebook. It will analyze the type of expertise you're best known for, your "reach," and the numbers of people who cite you, among a host of other metrics. Don't become obsessed, but Alan noted that when he increased his daily tweets from one to three (which he does at the same time, within 90 seconds), and was the guest interviewee of a Twitter "radio broadcast," his Klout score increased to over 60 (which is quite high).

Don't fritter or Twitter your life away, but do spend a small amount of time establishing an intelligent presence and marketing strategy. If Twitter is solely recreational for you, that's fine, but don't confuse that with marketing!

LinkedIn

So what is LinkedIn? It is simply a professional social network that has primarily a business focus (even though that sounds like an oxymoron). Unlike FB that has both a personal and business side to it, LinkedIn is supposedly all about the business side. (We will use the abbreviation LI to represent LinkedIn for this chapter.) And finally, since our book's focus is on helping you transform your business, we are going to ignore one of LI's other popular features, which is using it as a resume hub to get a job.

The way it works is that you create connections with other business professionals by inviting them to connect or you being invited. You and your connections are then categorized as level one connection. The connections then between you and their friends (who are not connected to you) are categorized as level two connections. And then the connection between you and the friend of the friend is categorized as a level three. See Figure 10.13.

As you may have noticed in Figure 10.13, LI indicates that we have over 10 million friends' connections. We have proposed public that if one can help us set up the structure for collecting 50 cents from each of our connections, we will split the revenues with you! That is to say, this figure is more theoretical than actual.

Your Network of Trusted Professionals

You are at the center of your network. Your connections can introduce you to 10,658,700+ professionals — here's how your network breaks down:

1	**Your Connections** Your trusted friends and colleagues	779
2	**Two degrees away** Friends of friends; each connected to one of your connections	303,000+
3	**Three degrees away** Reach these users through a friend and one of their friends	10,354,900+
	Total users you can contact through an Introduction	10,658,700+

108,727 new people in your network since July 18

Figure 10.13: **Connection levels**

Why should you consider joining and using LinkedIn?

Similar to the connections we have previously identified for other social media platforms, LI enables you to connect with business minds worldwide. LI offers advance search capabilities that enable you to locate individuals within organizations and then request to connect with them. This is one of LI's very powerful options.

LI enables you to ask questions in predetermined categories and get quick answers (see Figure 10.14). We've seen much better participation results from using LI compared to other social media platforms. You

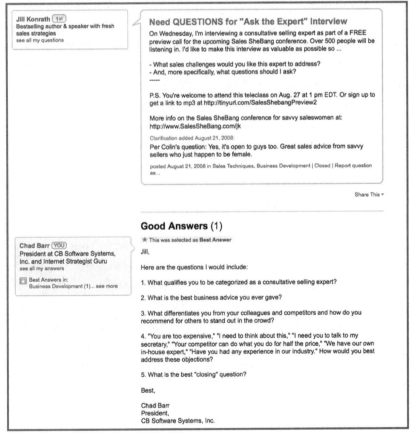

Figure 10.14: **LinkedIn questions and answers**

can also answer questions regarding topics in areas of your expertise and interest. You may search topics by several categories and then focus on the ones you like. This gives you exposure within the LI community and the possibility of positioning you as an expert and attracting professionals to contact you. The person who starts the question has the ability of ranking the best answer, which may also provide additional credibility to your profile. *Once you provide your answer, you may want to repurpose it on your blog or even create an article.* As individuals answer your questions and those of others, their profile information displays next to their answer and you may then want to connect with the ones you enjoy reading, and help.

Join and consider creating groups, which is the LI version of communities as we have discussed in great detail. If you have the elements required to create your own thriving community, we recommend you create your robust and branded community independent of LI and not host it on their platform. We do, however, highly encourage you to join groups where your expertise may shine and participate in their discussions. This is a great way to see what others are discussing, provide your wisdom, and start creating relationships. Also, don't underestimate that power of asking questions. The last thing you want to do is come across as the "professor." Figure 10.15 is an example of the Harvard Business Review group Chad belongs to.

You can share interesting information through your "Share an update" box and apply the concepts we've discussed about posting. Be valuable, provocative, and frequent, but do not spam.

Giving recommendations on LinkedIn is your way of giving back to your partners, colleagues, and clients. We can't comprehend when individuals are asking for our recommendations when we have not had any prior working relations with them. LinkedIn's recommendations-requesting technology makes it extremely easy to leverage in your business. Some of our clients struggle with solicitating of testimonials for their website. Why not use LI to help you do this? When you do so, not only will these recommendations

Figure 10.15: **LinkedIn group**

display on your LI profile page, but you may then incorporate them on your website. As easy as that.

When faced with an opportunity you cannot or do not want to handle, why not search your LI network and provide a recommendation to others who can use the business? They may just reciprocate one day. *Also, one of the best ideas we can think of is to help send business to your own clients.* LI enables you to see what your competitors are doing and embrace them. It is quite common for us to refer business we choose not to take on to individuals and organizations that are perceived to be our competitors.

As your profile information becomes available, it then also becomes available for search engines to find and index in their database. This improves your ranking and potential traffic to your sites.

Finally, LI is like a great digital "Rolodex"® tracking system. When individuals change positions (since you may be targeting executives in organizations), you will always have the latest way of connecting with them as soon as they update their LI profile. This way you don't have to worry that your own database may not be reflecting the latest change; you can use LI to occasionally update your other contact databases.

As is customary and required on the other social media platforms we've discussed, you must set up your profile so people can easily find you and learn about you. We don't want to waste time on the obvious, but your profile must focus on how you help improve your clients' conditions, a strong value proposition, and credible results.

Basically, what we have discussed in earlier chapters that helps create credibility on the web applies to your profile. Make sure that you add a professional photo of yourself and realize that you may include up to three links to your sites or your landing pages. One final tweak we recommend is that instead of using an LI default website description such as "Portfolio," you may want to override it and choose "Samples of Our Work" instead. Also, specify your Twitter name so people can easily connect with you there.

Virtual Reality

Focus on the aspects of social media platforms most relevant to boost your business, and not on other options simply because they are offered.

Another important point is under your settings, set up your public profile, which controls what the public sees. An important component is your friendly URL and the creation of the LI badge that can then be displayed on your blog. You are welcome to check out Chad's and Alan's blogs and connect with us on LI here: www.linkedin.com/in/chadbarrgroup and here: www.linkedin.com/in/alanweissphd.

With whom should you connect?

- Anyone who wants to connect with you or others who initiate the request to connect with you. However, they must be genuine and credible. Take a quick look at their profiles and you should be able to determine this in a matter of a few seconds.
- Clients and past clients.
- Prospective clients.
- Executives in organizations.
- Journalists.
- Colleagues and professional business acquaintances.
- Interesting individuals in groups you belong to and others asking and answering questions.
- Competitors.

If you decide to create your own group, you may be wondering where and to whom you should promote it?

- To the entire list identified above.
- To thought leaders, popular and famous bloggers.
- Through your sites and signature files.
- To and on other social media platforms.
- To and on other groups.

We recommend you override the default invitation request to make it look more personal. Here is an example:

Dear Jim,

I've noticed quite a few mutual friends and interests and I am looking forward to connecting, learning, and sharing.

Best, Chad

So why should you connect with as many individuals as possible? The answer is simple: Your message then has a better chance of finding a potential buyer or collaborator.

Another practical feature of LI is the ability to organize and categorize your database based on your own designated categories. For example, when you connect with a new individual, you may categorize them as client, prospect, colleague, or other designations.

One of the useful things about LI is its integration with several popular and powerful applications. Some of our favorites are:

- WordPress integration, which will interface your blog to LI so all your blog content populates on LI in the designated area.
- Twitter integration, which then populates your tweets onto LI.
- Your Amazon reading list, which enables you to specify your favorite books you have read. This is especially effective when specifying your own books.
- Events promotion, which are similar to the events concepts on FB as we've discussed earlier.

Similar to FB, another option you may find of interest is the ability to advertise on LI.

If you are planning on targeting and segmenting the LI database to search, find, and contact potential new clients, we recommend you upgrade your free LI account to one of their premium accounts. Currently, there are three upgrade options that would provide you with advanced search capabilities. For this purpose, we find this option quite powerful. Take a look at the screenshot in Figure 10.16. It shows us visiting the "Search Companies" section of LI. It shows that IBM, for example, has 898 people that are in our network (1st and 2nd connection level). *Once I locate a person I want to contact, I may email them directly by using the InMail option, which is a part of the premium service option (we have no financial interest in it). Or, if they are a level 2 connection, I may then ask to get introduced to them through a level 1 connection I may already have. I may also refine the search criteria on the left-hand side to provide me with*

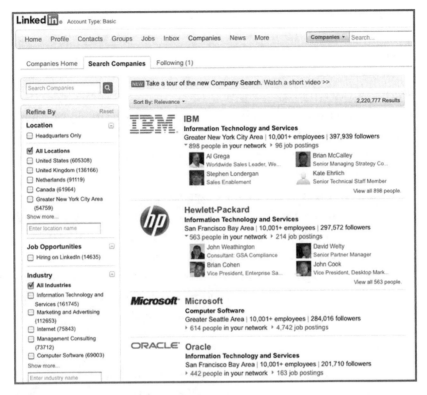

Figure 10.16: **Advance search for marketing**

further filtering capabilities. We suggest you experiment with these search options. You may surprise yourself.

LinkedIn can be useful IF you restrict yourself to legitimate business opportunities and marketing, and refrain from collecting links like some people collect stamps. Don't offer or provide recommendations and endorsements for those with whom you are not familiar.

Make this a serious, professional, and minimal time investment and you'll be maximizing your LinkedIn ROI.

And all the rest of the usual suspects

Considering our definition of social media at the beginning of this chapter, we would be remiss not to mention several other platforms that greatly impact connections and relationships. Therefore, we are going to reference the following platforms or tools under the social media category.

Blogs

Blogs have grown tremendously in their popularity, robustness, effectiveness, and ability to engage in conversations. The great ones have attracted a huge following where continual discussions are being conducted. If you are not convinced, just check out Alan's blog here: www.contrarianconsulting.com/blogs-facebook-twitter-and-chance and here: www.contrarianconsulting.com/blogs-facebook-twitter-and-chance/redux/ where he is poking at the social media world, attracting all its loyal supporters to come to its defense and "take on" Alan.

Are you leveraging your blog to attract a community around you, conduct meaningful discussions, and build trusting relationships? Are you willing to be provocative and even contrarian?

YouTube

One of the largest repositories of high-end intellectual property (that is, if you ignore all of the junk) as well as a great search engine tool, YouTube's social interface will help strengthen your brand not only by displaying your video content, but it will allow for visitors' comments and interactions with you and others. Have you created and promoted your YouTube channel yet? You can recycle your textual material into video here, getting twice the work out of the same intellectual property.

iTunes

iTunes is a remarkable place to share your intellectual property. Once it is integrated with your blog, all your podcasts will automatically be sent over to iTunes, making them accessible to audiences that may not know about you or your sites. Have you started your podcast recordings yet? Again, you can recycle text and video or vice versa.

Blog talk radio

This is another platform that enables you to easily record interviews with others that are then published on your site as well as integrated into iTunes.

eBay

eBay can absolutely be looked at as a social media platform. Known by your interest in and ability to purchase or sell products, it has its own communities of people looking for great buys.

Flickr

As well as being a photo-sharing site, Flickr can actually be leveraged as a great business tool to share and communicate about your photos with others, which will also allow for comments and feedback. Why not publish photos of your workshops and other events for your audience and community to enjoy?

Wikipedia

This popular online encyclopedia enables you to promote yourself and your brands while updating, communicating, and sharing with others. Have you looked into getting your profile there yet? It takes just a few minutes.

Apps

One of the hottest and fastest-growing phenomena, apps for mobile devices expose you and your brand to a huge audience that perhaps has yet to discover you. Is developing an app in your plans?

Bookmarking sites

Digg, StumbleUpon, and Delicious are attracting tremendous amounts of visitors who are looking for recommendations of what to click on and explore. They are all platforms you should consider embracing and leveraging into your business.

Skype

Although limited in the number of connections at one time, it enables you to connect multiple people into one video chat. Look at it as your private chat room, which could be a great business tool communicating with your clients and their teams. For quite a few years we and our clients have been using such technologies to communicate all over the globe in real time.

Mobile

This is where the action has been and it is expanding dramatically. For technologies to enable people to connect universally and continually, they must support all mobile devices. Are your sites displaying correctly on mobile devices?

Forums: www.AlansForums.com and www.AlanAndTheGang.com

We've left the best for last. These, from our perspective, are the ultimate social media experiences. We've been fortunate to successfully create, nurture, and grow probably the finest professional communities in the world. (One of Alan's trademarked phrases is "The Architect of Professional Communities™.") These sites are attracting some of the smartest minds worldwide with discussions on a multitude of fascinating topics. Have you thought about creating your own community by now? And why not join us?

How to guarantee a complete social media meltdown

- Exporting your social media connections to your database to email them your newsletters without their permission.
- Cursing and using poor and profane language.
- Spamming your audience.
- Overpromoting.
- Posting and sharing superfluous information or photos, and as our kids would say, TMI—too much information!

- Posting and sharing private information that may damage your reputation.
- Not posting useful content.
- Not engaging with your contacts and their comments.
- Listening to everyone claiming to be a social media expert.
- Attending to personal matters through your business profiles.
- Offending others with inappropriate religious, sexual, or political diatribes.
- Not replying rather quickly to defamatory accusations or other critique about you, your company, or your brands.

Some tough questions and considerations regarding social media

There is a fundamental truth that people will have to come to grips with: These sites are huge time dumps IF you allow them to be. They don't "amplify" anyone's message because they "amplify" ALL messages, meaning the cacophony is so intense that nothing stands out. The exceptions claiming business gains—we are talking making money, not making "contacts"—are rare and, frankly, we don't believe most of them.

But the key question, outside of spending a few minutes a day on social media, is: Am I better off, is my life enriched by the hours I spend on virtual social platforms each week, or is there something I'm not getting to, something I'm avoiding, something detracting from my growth?

When you challenge any aspect of the social platforms or act in a nonconformist way (e.g., Alan does not "follow" anyone on Twitter, though he has thousands of followers), you receive ripostes from the self-appointed owners of the secret decoder rings. They want to give you etiquette lessons. How can there be etiquette in what is, for all intents and purposes, a social free-for-all where most people don't care how they use the cutlery?

You can start some serious conversations on FB and elsewhere, but they peter out. Moreover, the amount of postings that have NO responses, NO commentaries, is huge, meaning that, well, perhaps no one among your "friends" cares! It's all about personal "air time" and being heard and seen, without having to be interesting, be helpful, or have new ideas.

There is a great tendency (and we are sad to say, audience acceptance) of people who dumb down the language. It's as if social media gives one the credence to talk incoherently and even use profane language. Our recommendation: STOP IT!

We do acknowledge that we have only scratched the surface when it comes to uncovering the vast potential of the internet. This also applies to social media, as the organizers and the users have not completely figured out how to leverage it in their businesses. What we do know is that it is evolving quickly and is becoming a newer and an additional way of creating relationships. So if you are targeting primarily consumers, many of them spend a lot of their time on social media and the key is to effectively reach them. Therefore, as you publish great and provocative

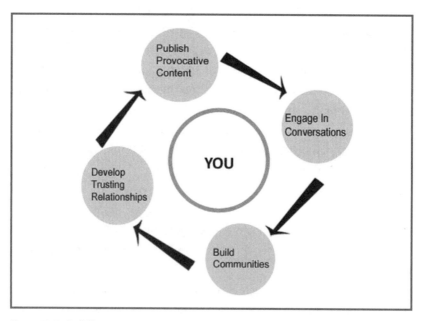

Figure 10.17: **Building your social media-based brand**

content, engage in conversations, and start creating communities and relationships, you will significantly strengthen your social media brand and attract them to you.

So where do you go from here? Imagine if you took the time you spent on social media and devoted it to writing a book, creating new intellectual property on your site, productizing your business, and developing new speeches? What would you say would have been the impact on your business in, say, one year? Our clients who have made these slight priority adjustments have seen outstanding results. You should be extremely selective and careful of your time there.

Social media action plan in 12 minutes or less per day

- Create a new blog and aim to post at least three times per week.
- Create your FB, LI, and Twitter profiles and possibly a FB business page, and design attractive Twitter and FB screens.
- Create a Bit.ly account to shorten your URL tweets.
- Start following others and accept requests to follow you.
- Integrate the social media platforms with each other and your blog.
- Tweet five times per week or more.
- Ask or answer three LI questions per week and repurpose your answers on your blog.
- Comment on other powerful bloggers' posts a few times per week.
- Engage in discussions whenever you can.

You can't see the entire British Museum, Disneyland, or the iTunes store in a single day, and the social media and related opportunities on the web are combinations of all three. Take your time, choose your spots, and be excellent at a few things, not mediocre at many.

The Future Foretold

we're always surprised by how stupid we were two weeks ago

The holographic web (well, almost)

As we write this, computers are creating three-dimensional models produced on special printers. This technology is in its infancy, but we suspect that everyone reading this book will live to see the equivalent of "tool and dye" work created on your personal computer.

The physical dimensionality will be paralleled by a virtual richness. Meetings will increasingly be conducted in settings where the other parties are only virtually in the room but very realistically present, in that they can be seen constantly against business backdrops similar to those of the other party, and in some cases a continuation of it. There will be no more dozing off or flying paper airplanes while the boss is talking about strategy.

Figures 11.1 to 11.3 feature the virtual office of Alan's partner in The Odd Couple® speaking workshops, Patricia Fripp.

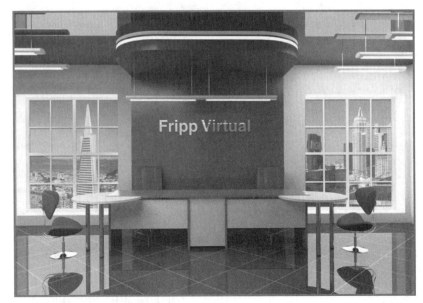

Figure 11.1: **Fripp's "reception area"**

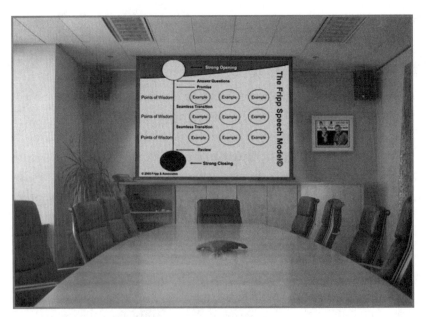

Figure 11.2: **The "conference room"**

Figure 11.3: **A "study area"**

As you can see, Fripp (as she prefers to be called) has created an entire environmental experience for her online virtuality. (You can visit her here: www.fripp.com/blog/tag/virtual-office/.)

Virtual Reality

The multi-dimensionality was missing from virtual meetings, but that is being overcome, and actual travel to distant sites will decrease substantially.

We believe that the threats caused by international instability, the discomfort caused by airline security, and the rapacious and unceasing attempts by the airlines to collect money for everything short of a life vest will stimulate virtual holographic meetings. While they may not reach the Star Trek nature of spectral images created in the room, they will provide a realistic, *and more importantly, real time*, experience for all participants.

Imagine this used for:

· Performance evaluations for remote personnel.
· Ongoing professional development (instead of dreadful, tedious, cumbersome "webinars").
· Sales calls that can be set up quickly, between other priorities, and with the key people available.
· Interviews, which are recorded for rebroadcast.
· Observations of actual work being done, be it assembling an engine, contacting a customer, or performing heart surgery.

Those are just a few examples. Alan's gourmet treks have taken him and his wife to famed chef Thomas Keller's two brilliant establishments, Per Se in New York, and The French Laundry in Yountville, California. A kitchen tour of each revealed a closed circuit television operation allowing Mr. Keller to closely observe his other kitchen from whichever one he happened to actually be in.

You should be building this into your *Million Dollar Web Presence* plans. Think about your ability to interact with prospects and clients in real time and in simulated three dimensions. Your global growth should be turbo-charged by this kind of capability and, we hope, ingenuity on your part.

As we write this, we have scheduled workshops that will feature live streaming video around the world with the ability of distant participants to ask questions, occupy "hot seats," and be normally involved. (And we'll have a "Twitter Gallery" of people tweeting as we proceed.)

This is a future easy to foretell.

Dick Tracey had it right

For those of you of a certain age, you can remember when Dick Tracey was one of the hottest comic strip characters around. There was a curious mix of science fiction in his detective work, and one of his primary tools was a wrist radio. In fact, whenever he held up his wrist to talk to someone, the cartoonist drew in a cue with "wrist radio" and an arrow pointing to the device, since it was so incredibly absurd at the time.

Today, of course, the iPhone IS the wrist radio, except it does more, and Mr. Tracey would have been amazed at his increased effectiveness.

The iPhone is the grandson of the Walkman, invented by Akio Morita of Sony, who was told by his engineers and marketers that no one was seeking a device to wear on their belt in order to listen to music through earphones. (Everyone was going to boom boxes and big speakers.) He told them they would soon need it and, besides, he owned the place.

We remind you of all this because while Tracey might not have begun in our lifetimes, the Walkman did for many of you, and the iPhone has for all of you. That's how fast things can change these days. Tracey was created by Chester Gould who foresaw the "wrist radio" by decades, but the Walkman was created only in 1979 and the iPhone in about 2007 (depending upon to whom you listen).

Thus, we're confident telling you that the immediate years ahead will probably see the following developments:

- The ability to call someone and look at common images, be they web pages, photos, graphics, or even hand-drawn images.
- Multiple-party, face-to-face calling.
- Storage that updates the very last keystroke on every platform you have and/or choose to share with others. The latest Apple operating system, Lion, automatically saves everything without prompts, and apps such as Dropbox duplicate everything you include across all platforms, including shared platforms.
- Tiny ear buds that work wirelessly with a communications device kept elsewhere (in a pocket or even a desk), allowing for very private communications (and eliminating the ridiculous chunk of blinking metal that some people walk around with at the moment).

- The ability to call up a specific web destination and view it or even print it on a local printer wirelessly, or a small printer that fits in a briefcase or handbag.
- The ability to include, in real time, breaking developments on your website or blog, using photos and text from mobile devices (rather primitive apps allow for some of this now).
- Universal, high-quality contact that will make current "dropped calls" or Skype technical issues seem like the old black-and-white TV days.
- Priority intercepts that will allow designated special people (family members, key clients, emergency personnel) override your "lockouts" and contact you in case of emergency or vital business.

We'd also like to take a moment here to talk about what we see as the evolution of what we've been calling the social media platforms.

Virtual Reality

The test of technology is "smaller/cheaper." If mechanisms become both smaller and cheaper, they are here to stay. Market competition will ensure the highest level of effectiveness.

We foresee a stratification of social media platforms into legitimate and focused "social" purposes and separate, legitimate, and focused "business" purposes. It makes zero sense to us to entrust marketing to milieus where someone is trying to sell life insurance, someone else is trying to get a date, and someone else is attempting to find a strategy client. It's like walking into a bar and expecting to find a prospective buyer *who would consider doing business with someone who expects to find clients in a bar!* (Most people aren't even effective getting a date in a bar, and the only thing you can rely upon is getting a drink if you pay for it.)

Facebook, at the moment, is simply Twitter with more character spaces allowed. LinkedIn is so vast that it's not as personal as simply cold-calling prospects. (We love the nerve of people on LinkedIn who are total strangers but ask us to "endorse" or recommend them!) However, these organizations are being valued in the billions of dollars, and they're going to have to be made more pragmatic in terms of pleasing advertisers (who are now supplying almost all the revenue) and investors, let alone members.

Consequently, we envision a variety of social and business platforms from which to choose, some of which may be membership-only. After all, the web is the repository of the highest level of content-specific information that exists. (Want to find rare New Zealand stamps or left-handed fly fishing gear? Just use Google.)

At the moment, the party is too large and noisy, and someone left the door open. There's no telling who's next to you and it's hard to get a key person's attention because when you amplify *everything* all you create is a cacophony, not a standout sound.

You'll be able to create a dynamic and singular web presence by focusing on those prospects who best constitute your most important markets.

In the graph shown in Figure 11.4 on page 262, you can see what this might look like, and why it's somewhat counterintuitive. You shouldn't be concerned with the great mass of people in the middle, but solely those on the right, who are your most important prospective buyers. The "third dimension" to our chart illustrates what most people seeking web dominance miss: It's not about "hits" or how many open a newsletter, or "traffic." It's about penetration of your most desirable prospects.

You're better off with 15 percent of your high-potential market than 40 percent of an indifferent and/or irrelevant market. This is what the future holds in store: the ability to designate, isolate, and penetrate *those prospects which are most likely to purchase in the largest amounts.*

We've pointed out earlier that current computerized technology is the latest iteration of Gutenberg's moveable type. Let's examine why that is.

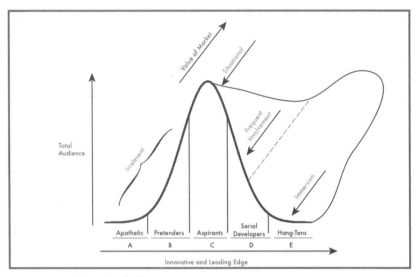

Figure 11.4: **Market value bell curve**

Why the iPhone is the best thing since Gutenberg

The internet arose (irrespective of Al Gore) as an attempt for the U.S. military to gain superiority over their USSR counterparts. When first adopted by business, the web was really just an extended business card, sort of cardboard on steroids: some text and limited imaging. That was the one-dimensional web.

Two-dimensionality followed with Skype, online meetings, teleconferencing, and so forth, to the "holographic" point we made about the present and coming three-dimensionality. Since digital imaging of people is now a reality, virtual reality may be replaced by "synthetic reality," with realism as it never appeared before.

The iPhone and iPad, accompanied by mobile and wifi technologies, allows near-constant connection to the internet, which will soon be an unbroken connection, no less than the electrical grid; that includes 40,000 feet in the air, in tunnels, under water, and deep within buildings.

The proliferation of apps has created what Alan has coined as REV: reciprocating, exponential value. The more apps, the greater the appeal, the more people are attracted, the more the device (iPhone) is improved, the more apps are created—and so forth. We're seeing the digital, cyberspace version of the heretofore impossible "perpetual motion machine." There are other platforms and other PDA devices, but the iPhone has been THE invention to revolutionize not merely how we communicate, *but how we behave.*

Virtual Reality

How much more productive are you today than before the advent of the iPhone? Soon, no one born will know what it is like NOT to have an iPhone (wrist radio)!

In late 2011, there are about 90 million apps *downloaded every day, globally.* The amount of information and the way in which we process it is exponentially growing. It's not merely information any more that's the key, it's how we act and behave. Recently, a computer from IBM defeated contestants in the game show *Jeopardy* (where Alan once appeared and lost to a dancing waiter from Iowa). All but the very best grandmasters lose to computers in chess, and that will soon change. Test your children (or yourself) on doing math in your head—you're not as good as you once were, because you've come to rely on computing power in place of brainpower for mundane tasks.

Now add in voice recognition, facial recognition, automated GPS, tailored apps for specific needs, and we're at a point where we merely can say, "Excellent cabernet under $300 with fine steaks, within five miles," and the phone or car will lead us there while making a reservation simultaneously.

Gutenberg enabled masses to read. First it was the Bible, so that they needn't be dependent on their clergy and Latin, and then it was the news, so that they needn't be dependent on hearsay and superstition.

They could relate to people in other places and in other conditions. They became self-aware.

Margaret Wheatley, in her excellent book *Leadership and the New Science*, contends that animals have different levels of consciousness because they process information at different rates. Hence, a dog has a higher level of consciousness than a snail, because a dog processes more information.

We apply that to humans, as well. Some people process information faster and better than others, and thus have a higher level of consciousness—they are more aware of their surroundings, faster to act, more likely to be opportunistic in response to events. Traditionally, we've called that "smarts," or "luck," or even "a gift." Today, we can see that the appropriate use of technology can lead to higher consciousness.

This is no small issue—it is life-changing. The potential represented by an iPhone and its apps (which we're using here as a metaphor for all technology because it is a forerunner) can transform human consciousness through the faster and higher-quality processing of information. Guesswork is gone with Wikipedia; laborious search is gone with Google; the toil of creating relationships is gone with social media platforms.

However, as with anything else, the ultimate result is determined by the expertise of the user. Hence, we've spent the preponderance of our time in this book trying to help you utilize this enormous change agent called the web with alacrity, comfort, and discrimination.

If you learn well and are bold in your use, you will be able to take a call from a client, find the key document to reference, send the critical information, watch the client's reaction, accept a new project, and process the payment—all while on your iPhone or iPad *while reclining on the beach*. (See applications such as LINKVT https://tf.lynk-systems.com, which provide online processing from almost any platform right now.) The analogy to those people learning to read post-Johannes Gutenberg is very apt to all of us learning to live post-Steve Jobs! Gutenberg didn't merely enable reading, he changed society and civilization.

And that's what we're seeing today, as well. The future foretold is a future of continuing access, not merely instant access, and a power that has never been harnessed before. The old bromide that a current issue of *The New York Times* has more information to be processed than someone in the 16th century processed in an entire lifetime has never been validated and is a modern myth. But we are all processing—and more important, utilizing—information today at a rate unheard of even 20 years ago.

But John Naisbitt had it right 30 years ago in *Megatrends: The New Directions Transforming Our Lives*. Everything depends on how well you use the power. There's a huge difference between being on Facebook three hours a day and simply chatting, and being on it for 20 minutes a day and building your business. Our thrust here is web dominance, not recreation or entertainment, which we trust you can find for yourself.

The power represented by the iPhone as metaphor is sufficient to change your world right now. But the point isn't how many apps you have, but do you have the apps that are right for you? Are you focused merely on the technology, or on the growth of your business, practice, or company? Technology, even when available and useful 24 hours a day, is never an end in itself, any more than electricity is an end in itself.

It is the power to accomplish other things.

Time travel

We wouldn't be responsible without alerting you—perhaps admonishing you—about the tremendous time-dump potential existing in social media as it is now constituted. Here is some work that Alan did as a lark, which prompted a vituperous response on his blog:

> This is an unscientific, undocumented, and probably unpopular analysis of what I'm learning as King of Social Media. (I'm reminded of a great review of a leading actor in *King Lear* by Eugene Field: "He played the king as though under momentary apprehension that someone else was about to play the ace.")

Here are my anecdotal observations.

If people visit LinkedIn twice a day for 15 minutes each time, that's 2.5 hours in a five-day week. (I'm discounting weekends, though I shouldn't, because social media wandering is clearly a full-time avocation, but I want to be conservative here.)

If they visit Facebook four times a day for 10 minutes each, that's roughly 3.3 hours.

If they Twitter six times a day for five minutes each time, that 2.5 hours. (Or 12 times at 2.5 minutes each—you get the idea.)

If they post on their blogs three times a week (rather important to keep a blog active and interesting), and the creation and posting of the item take 30 minutes (and I think I'm really low-balling this one), that's 2.5 hours.

And now I'm going to add just two hours to the week, that accommodate reading others' blogs, replying to commentary, following up social media stuff off-line, updating profiles, uploading photos, and so on.

Drum roll, please: We now have a five-day week on a conventional 40-hour basis with about 13 hours engaged in what is somewhat inappropriately termed "social media." I understand that those hours may well extend into evening or early morning time. On the basis of a 40-hour week, that's 33 percent devoted to this stuff; but even on the basis of a 12-hour day, the percentage is 22 percent.

If you were devoting less than half those 13 hours, say, six hours, to other professional marketing pursuits, I estimate you could do any one of the following during that week:

- Write two to three chapters of a book.
- Create and post 10 to 12 position papers on your website.
- Call, at a moderate pace, to follow up with 30 past clients and/or warm leads.
- Send out a dozen press releases.
- Engage in a full day of self-development or a workshop.
- Create three speeches or a complete multi-day workshop.

- Create a new product to be sold on your website.
- Create, and develop a marketing plan for, a teleconference.
- Create and record three podcasts.
- Create and tape a video.
- Contact 30 prior clients for testimonials, referrals, or references.
- Attend two networking events.
- Create and distribute two newsletters.
- Complete at least half of a professional book proposal for an agent.
- Respond to 50 or more reporters' inquiries on, say, PRLeads.com.
- Seek out two high-potential *pro bono* opportunities.
- Contact and follow up with five trade associations for speaking opportunities.

You get the idea. Don't forget, in my unscientific analysis, I've halved the hours I think are really being invested in full-fledged social media activity based on an already conservative estimate of what they truly are. And I'm not even counting other networks or platforms, just the four I've mentioned.

And over the course of a couple of months, you can easily do ALL of the bullet points, if you have a mind to do so. I'm just allocating six hours a week, just over an hour a day.

My current evaluation is this: Don't confuse occupation with avocation. I've never said that "social media" is evil or will not help someone find a buyer somewhere at some time. Heck, I've become an avid blogger, and I visit Facebook and now Twitter daily. Yet I can still do all of the bullet points above and work only 20 hours a week.

If you're serious about corporate consulting and coaching, and the blog you are currently visiting IS located at www.contrarianconsulting.com, then I'd continue to advise that you're not going to find those buyers on social platforms. Is it impossible? No. Have some people done it? They claim so. But if you're engaged in social browsing at the EXPENSE of those bullet points, then that's not a good disposition nor apportionment of time. If you can do both, and still live a balanced and fulfilling life by your terms, then go for it.

I'm posting intellectual property, for free of course, on Twitter, just as I do here. I do find that these platforms present a great way to pay back, to contribute, and to share. You have to be judicious in your selections, however, since some people just want "air time" and you only have so much air.

There, that's done!

We predict a level of transparency and connectivity that will parallel movie revolutions such as *Avatar* in digital form. We said in the introduction to the book:

We'll help you immediately translate your intellectual capital into intellectual property, and then accelerate its dissemination; leverage the web to enable your highest potential buyers to immediately realize your worth; and move you to a global presence faster than you can move to the next state or province.

Technology is moving from an implementation alternative to a strategic consideration in creating business's futures. That is, technology will determine products, services, and relationships. That's why you need a million-dollar web presence, because it will create a dynamic and fulfilling strategy.

We hope you can see the power and reach of the web, and appreciate the potential of your own web presence. We believe you can readily build that into a multi-million-dollar business.

We know, because we have. Thanks for joining us on this journey.

About the Authors

Chad Barr

Born and raised in Israel, Chad came to the United States at age 22 determined to capture the American dream. In 1991, that dream came true when Chad started his own company CB Software Systems. CB Software Systems and The Chad Barr Group, have attracted organizations that span the globe and include clients in Italy, Germany, UK, Australia, New Zealand, Canada and the United States.

Chad is an internet and business strategist, and a mentor, who successfully guides and helps his clients leverage the web to transform their businesses by combining technologies such as websites, blogs, newsletters, surveys, apps, social media tools, and other innovative platforms with effective strategy and tactics.

Chad devotes much of his time writing, coaching, consulting, speaking, heading his company, and pursuing its vision. He has published over 100 articles and continues to share his vision worldwide. Chad helps create some of the finest professional communities around the globe. His firm, The Chad Barr Group, is recognized as one of the leading internet development organizations in the world.

He also enjoys his latest passion as grandfather to two wonderful, (and of course, brilliant), grandchildren. Having also been a professional guitarist, his grandchildren think he is the coolest guitarist in the world.

Alan Weiss

Alan Weiss is one of those rare people who can say he is a consultant, speaker and author and mean it. His consulting firm, Summit Consulting Group, Inc. has attracted clients such as Merck, Hewlett-Packard, GE, Mercedes-Benz, State Street Corporation, Times Mirror Group, The Federal Reserve, The New York Times Corporation, and over 500 other leading organizations.

His speaking typically includes 30 keynotes a year at major conferences, and he has been a visiting faculty member at over seven notable universities. He is an inductee into the Professional Speaking Hall of Fame® and the concurrent recipient of the National Speakers Association Council of Peers Award of Excellence, representing the top 1 percent of professional speakers in the world. He has been named a Fellow of the Institute of Management Consultants, one of only two people in history holding both those designations.

His prolific publishing includes over 500 articles and 44 books. *Success* magazine cited him in an editorial devoted to his work as "a worldwide expert in executive education." *The New York Post* called him "one of the most highly regarded independent consultants in America."

He is the recipient of the Lifetime Achievement Award of the American Press Institute, the first-ever for a non-journalist, and one of only seven awarded in the 65-year history of the association. He once appeared on the popular American TV game show *Jeopardy*, where he lost badly in the first round to a dancing waiter from Iowa.

Index